IRELAND
POCKET GUIDE

◉ Walking Eye App

Your Insight Pocket Guide purchase includes a free download of the destination's corresponding eBook. It is available now from the free Walking Eye container app in the App Store and Google Play. Simply download the Walking Eye container app to access the eBook dedicated to your purchased book. The app also features free information on local events taking place and activities you can enjoy during your stay, with the option to book them. In addition, premium content for a wide range of other destinations is available to purchase in-app.

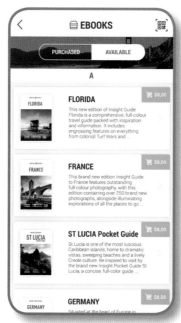

HOW TO DOWNLOAD THE WALKING EYE APP

Available on purchase of this guide only.
1. Visit our website: www.insightguides.com/walkingeye
2. Download the Walking Eye container app to your smartphone (this will give you access to your free eBook and the ability to purchase other products)
3. Select the scanning module in the Walking Eye container app
4. Scan the QR Code on this page – you will be asked to enter a verification word from the book as proof of purchase
5. Download your free eBook* for travel information on the go

* Other destination apps and eBooks are available for purchase separately or are free with the purchase of the Insight Guide book

TOP **10** ATTRACTIONS

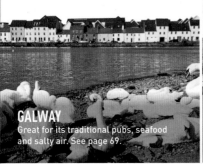

GALWAY
Great for its traditional pubs, seafood and salty air. See page 69.

DINGLE PENINSULA
This idyllic area lives up to visitors' romantic notions of Ireland. See page 64.

GLENDALOUGH
An ancient monastery in a spectacular setting. See page 44.

BOOK OF KELLS
Trinity College, Dublin, houses this wonderful product of Ireland's heritage. See page 28.

NEWGRANGE
These burial chambers represent a major feat of prehistoric engineering. See page 40.

CORK CITY
The Republic's second city has an old-fashioned charm. See page 55.

CROWN LIQUOR SALOON
Great tiles and cosy snugs in Belfast's foremost pub. See page 83.

DONEGAL
The countryside and coastline here have a wild beauty. See page 79.

GRAFTON STREET
Dublin's shopping artery has a continental air. See page 28.

TEMPLE BAR
The lively hub of Dublin's nightlife. See page 34.

A PERFECT TOUR

Day 1

Dublin
Walk the streets of Georgian Dublin, from Trinity College's cobbled quadrangle to the wide expanse of Merrion Square, then enjoy a light lunch at the National Gallery. Cross the Ha'penny Bridge and follow O'Connell Street to Parnell Square and the Dublin Writers Museum.

Day 3

Cork City
Explore Cork's city centre on foot, lunching in the vast covered food market. Then take a 20-minute train ride to the port of Cobh, the last sight of home for generations of emigrants, whose tale is told at The Queenstown Story in Cobh Heritage Centre.

Day 4

Coast path to Killarney
The west Cork coastal road (N71) meanders through tiny villages where the pubs showcase local artisan foods, to the treasure-packed Bantry House and sub-tropical Glengarriff. Drive through Kenmare to Moll's Gap for a jaw-dropping scenic approach to Killarney.

Day 2

Kilkenny and Tipperary
Leave Dublin by car for Kilkenny, founded by St Canice in the 6th century, and Kilkenny Castle, a magnificent edifice in rich parkland beside the River Nore. Have lunch at the Kilkenny Design Centre, an emporium of Irish crafts. Drive on to Tipperary and climb the Rock of Cashel, to savour its magnificent ruins.

Day 5 & 6

Kerry
Explore the lakes and heather-clad mountains of Killarney. The Gap of Dunloe excursion includes a lake cruise, join it at Ross Castle.

Day 8

The wild west

Drive west from Galway to Connemara, a sparsely populated wilderness of bog, scattered blue lakes and distant purple mountains. Enjoy the seafood in Clifden, then head for the Connemara National Park, and walk up Diamond Hill for a panoramic view.

Day 10

Belfast

An impressive Victorian city with chic bars and restaurants, and quirky museums and libraries, Belfast is a popular weekend break destination, with friendly locals, known for their down-to-earth sense of humour. Visit Titanic Belfast, the world's largest Titanic visitor attraction, to explore the history of the Titanic, and understand the local pride in the city's industrial past.

Day 7

Cliffs of Moher

At Lahinch, you can surf the same Atlantic breakers that pound the nearby Cliffs of Moher. Warm up with Irish stew in Doolin while foot-tapping to live Irish music, and consider a day trip to the Aran Islands, or a visit to the Burren's numerous megalithic remains.

Day 9

The Antrim Coast

Wonder at the Giant's Causeway's bizarre basalt columns, as have generations of visitors. Enjoy the cosy inn at Bushmills (see page 106), next door to Ireland's oldest distillery. Nearby are the romantic ruins of Dunluce Castle, perched on a clifftop.

CONTENTS

INTRODUCTION

The grass really does grow greener in Ireland – it's not called the 'Emerald Isle' for nothing, although the rain-drenched verdant pastures alternate with plains of grain, bleak and rugged hills, mountains and soggy bogs. The quick-changing sky adds to the drama of the encounter between land and sea. You will never be further than 115km (70 miles) from Ireland's dramatic 4,800-km (3,000-mile) coastline. Far to the west lies America, a beacon for countless emigrants during the 19th century. To the east lies Britain, whose relationship with its next-door neighbour has for 800 years been one of the most sensitive and complex in European geopolitics.

The Cliffs of Moher in Co Clare

The proximity of the Gulf Stream keeps winters mild. Snow is rare, rain is not. Significant rainfall is recorded on three out of every four days near the west coast, and on every second day in the east, and ranges from stormy torrents to refreshing mist so nebulous that it leaves the pavement unmarked. The sun is never far behind the rain, however, and the slightest shower has always been a fine excuse for an Irish rainbow.

There are, of course, two Irelands: the 26 counties of the Republic of Ireland (Éire) and the six counties of Northern Ireland. This gives the island two capitals: Dublin and Belfast, each with their own governments. In Dublin, a lively city of broad avenues, green parks and harmonious, ordered terraces, there is more in the way of museums, galleries and other cultural attractions than in many cities of comparable size, plus a delightfully subversive sense of humour. In contrast, Belfast

Emigration

Around 6.4 million people live on the island – fewer than before the great potato famine of the 1840s. Emigration was high until the 'Celtic Tiger' boom, when jobs in new industries kept locals at home. With the bleaker economic outlook people are leaving again.

is Ireland's industrial centre and its energy is more grounded and less subtle than Dublin's.

By and large, though, the truly inspiring sights of Ireland are found outside the big towns. Ireland is still rooted in agriculture and, as you travel by car or bus from one town to the next, you will pass through miles of farmland generously populated with sheep and cattle. Natural wonders in Ireland can be as awesome as the Cliffs of Moher, or as tranquil as the Lakes of Killarney; as mystical as the holy mountain of Croagh Patrick, or as delightful as the horse-breeding pastures of the Curragh. Scattered amidst these natural beauties stand impressive stone relics which date back thousands of years. In Ireland, the concept of a town is not much more than a thousand years old. Before then, the island was almost entirely rural, and its now ancient buildings often began as monastic settlements that kept learning alive in Europe during the Dark Ages.

This is a small country but it's one to savour slowly. A signpost may present you with three ways of getting to a destination, or it may show none. Ask a passer-by, and they'll probably reassure you that it's 'just down the road' because they won't wish to distress you by telling you it's really 32km (20 miles) along a narrow, twisting road.

THE IRISH

More than 1.8 million people live in and around Dublin, the largest city in the Republic of Ireland and home to almost a third of its population. Belfast, with a population of around 670,000, is the hub of Northern Ireland, which has remained a part of the United Kingdom when the island was partitioned after the Irish War of Independence. The new republic, whose birth pangs in 1922 included a civil war, settled down to being a predominantly rural economy, with social affairs and its education system strongly influenced by the Catholic church.

In the final quarter of the 20th century, as Northern Ireland was suffering political turmoil, the South set about transforming itself into a modern European state. Membership of the European Union provided great economic benefits, and tax incentives were strategically used to attract European and American industries, primarily in the high-tech and pharmaceutical sectors. A strong youth culture turned Dublin into a party town targeted for weekend breaks by Europe's budget airlines.

Where there's smoke

The characteristic smell of peat fires pervades much of Ireland's countryside. Since the 17th century the bogs have been exploited as an inexpensive source of fuel. During the great potato famine (1845–51) dried peat was often the only fuel available. In recent times, more efficient methods of cutting the peat have put an extra strain on Irish bogs and, although peat fires smell lovely in winter, the remaining bogs are to be protected from further digging.

A NATIVE TONGUE

The historic Anglo-Norman conquest of Ireland in 1169 paved the way for the supremacy of the English language over Gaelic. According to the 2011 census, 1.7 million people speak the Irish language, with varying degrees of fluency. Reviving Gaelic – or Irish, as it is usually called, has become state policy; it is

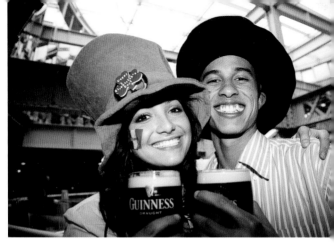

Enjoying the Guinness Storehouse

taught in schools and printed (along with English) on all official signs and documents. Indeed, in some Gaelic-speaking (Gaeltacht) areas, road signs are in Gaelic only, which can make life difficult for tourists. Irish-medium schools are increasingly popular in both urban and rural Ireland, bringing the Irish language outside of its traditional heartland. Its vocabulary, intonation and sentence structures have infiltrated the English spoken here, creating great literature and lending everyday speech a touch of poetry.

THE NORTHERN COUNTIES

For the last three decades of the 20th century, the image of Northern Ireland has been tarnished by an ugly sectarian conflict, known as "The Troubles", between Protestant Unionists and Catholic Republicans. Today, although animosities can still be ignited, a somewhat tetchy harmony prevails. Residents are down-to-earth and friendly (towards outsiders, anyway) and the scenery is spectacular, with some of the island's must-see sights.

A BRIEF HISTORY

Stone-Age relics reveal that Ireland has been inhabited for at least 8,000 years. The first settlers probably travelled on foot from Scandinavia to Scotland – England was linked at that time to northern Europe by land – then across what was a narrow sea gap to Ireland.

During the late Stone Age, inhabitants began to settle down and farm. Tombs and temples from this period can be found across the country. These monuments may be simple stone tripods in the middle of a farmer's field, or they can be sophisticated passage-graves built on astronomical principles and decorated with mysterious spiral and zigzag engravings.

New settlers introduced Bronze-Age skills from Europe, but by the time of the Iron Age Ireland was lagging behind the Continent. This technology did not reach the island until the last years of the pre-Christian era, thanks to Celtic tribes from central Europe.

The Roman legions that rolled across Western Europe into Britain stopped short at the Irish Sea. The island was left free to develop its own way of life during the centuries of the great Roman Empire. Though Irish society was decentralised into scores of bickering mini-kingdoms, a single culture did develop. Druids and poets told legends in a common language that is clearly recognisable as an early form of the Irish language, which later gave rise to Scots Gaelic and Manx.

A saint's success

St Patrick's crusade was a unique triumph. Ireland was the only Western European country where the local people were converted without a single Christian being martyred.

ST PATRICK'S DAY

The Celts frequently staged raids on Roman Britain for booty and slaves. During one 5th-century raid, they rounded up a large number of captives to ease the manpower shortage. One of these 'immigrants', a 16-year-old boy named Patrick, later became Ireland's national saint. After spending a few years as a humble shepherd, he escaped to Gaul, became a monk, and finally returned to convert 'the heathens' to Christianity.

St Patrick and his successors developed a system of monasteries to serve as the centre for all church activities. This suited life in Ireland – a rural and scantly populated island. While the rest of Europe crawled through the Dark Ages, the Irish monasteries kept the

Ireland's Viking heritage is remembered in Dublin

flame of Western culture alight. Scholarly minds from different regions of Europe converged on the island to participate in its religious and intellectual life. The monks from the 'island of saints and scholars' created beautiful illuminated manuscripts while others travelled to Britain and mainland Europe, founding monasteries abroad.

THE VIKINGS

At the turn of the 9th century, well-armed warriors sailed in from Scandinavia aboard sleek boats. The undefended Irish monasteries, full of relics and treasures, were easy targets. The shallow-draught ships moved in and attacked virtually at will, making their way around the Irish coast and up its rivers as well.

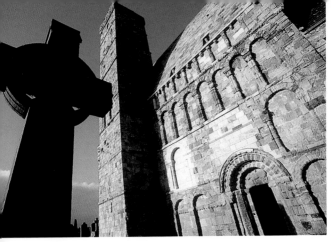
Pretty stone churches can be found in every town

This danger inspired multi-storey 'round towers', which variously served as watchtowers, belfries, storehouses, and places of refuge. The remains of 65 round towers still stand. But plunder wasn't the only thing on the Viking agenda: they soon added trading colonies around the coast and founded the first towns on the rural island – Dublin, Waterford and Limerick.

The Irish learned sailing, weaponry and metalworking from the Norse, but resented their presence. In the end, the natives ousted the Vikings, with the last struggle taking place in 1014 at the Battle of Clontarf, when the High King of Ireland, Brian Ború, defeated the tough Norse and their Irish allies, although he himself was killed in the battle.

RIVALRY AND REVENGE

Ireland's next invasion was motivated by jealousy. In 1152, the wife of Tiernan O'Rourke, an Irish warrior king, was carried off by rival Dermot MacMurrough of Leinster. Allegedly the lady was a willing victim, possibly even the instigator. Regardless, O'Rourke got his queen back a few months later, but wasn't about to forgive and forget. He forced Dermot to flee, in 1166, first to England and then France. But from there, Dermot was able to shape an alliance with a powerful Norman nobleman, the Earl of Pembroke. The Earl, known as Strongbow, agreed to lead an army to sweep Dermot back to power. In exchange, the Earl was to be given the hand of Dermot's daughter and the right to succeed him to the Leinster throne. The hardy Normans – the elite of Europe's warriors – won the Battle of Waterford in 1169, and Strongbow married his princess in Waterford's grand cathedral.

In further engagements, the Norman war machine stunned and swiftly defeated Norse and Irish forces. Things were going so well for Strongbow that his overlord, King Henry II of England, arrived in 1171 to assert his sovereignty.

THE ENGLISH ASCENDANCY

The Anglo-Norman occupation brought profound and long-lasting changes. Towns, churches and castles were built alongside institutions for feudal government. There was much resentment among the Irish, but for the colonial rulers the challenge of revolt was less serious than the danger of total cultural assimilation. With settlers adopting the ways of the natives, rather than the other way round, the Statutes of Kilkenny were introduced in 1366, banning intermarriage and forbidding the English from speaking Gaelic.

English control was consolidated when the House of Tudor turned its attention to Ireland. Henry VIII, the first English monarch to be titled 'King of Ireland', introduced the Reformation to Ireland as well as England, but the new religion of Protestantism took root only in the Pale (the area around Dublin) and in the large provincial towns under English control. In the rest of Ireland, Catholic monasteries carried on as before, as did the Irish language.

Emigration statue, County Cork

From the mid-16th century, the implementation of the so-called plantation policy heralded the large-scale redistribution of wealth. Desirable farmland was confiscated from Catholics and given to Protestant settlers. During the Reign of Elizabeth I revolts were widespread, but the most unyielding resistance was in the northeastern province of Ulster, where chiefs formed an alliance with Spain – the Queen's bitterest enemy. In 1601, a Spanish mini-armada sailed into the southern port of Kinsale. The English defeated the invaders and the Ulstermen who attempted to join them. Leading Ulster aristocrats, now defeated, abandoned their land for European exile. The 'plantation' programme continued fitfully. During the reign of James I, most of the northern land was confiscated and 'planted' with thousands of Scots and English, who changed the face of the province. After the English Civil War, Oliver Cromwell, England's ruler, ruthlessly massacred the garrisons at Drogheda and Wexford as the price for their support of Charles I, and pursued his own colonisation of Ireland. From 1654, Catholics were only allowed to hold land west of the River Shannon, much of it scarcely habitable. 'To Hell or to Connaught' was the slogan used to sum up the alternatives for the dispossessed.

After the religious war that culminated in the Battle of the Boyne, the Irish Catholic majority was subjected to further persecution in the form of the Penal Laws, introduced by the all-Protestant Irish parliament and designed to keep Catholics away from positions of power and influence.

REVOLUTIONARY IDEAS

It took the American Revolution to provoke daring new thinking in Ireland. Henry Grattan led agitation for greater freedom and tolerance. A Protestant of aristocratic heritage, he staunchly defended the rights of all Irishmen in the House of Commons. Further pressure came from an Irish Protestant, Theobald Wolfe Tone, a young lawyer campaigning for parliamentary reform and the abolition of anti-Catholic laws. In 1793 Catholic landholders won the vote and other concessions thanks to Tone. In 1798 a French squadron came to the aid of Tone's United Irishmen off the coast of Cork. It was swiftly intercepted by British naval forces and Wolfe Tone was captured. Convicted of treason, he slit his throat before his sentence of death by hanging could be carried out.

In 1801 the Irish Parliament voted itself out of business by approving the Act of Union which established the United Kingdom of Great Britain and Ireland. All Irish MPs would now

BATTLE OF THE BOYNE

Ireland became the battleground for an English power struggle when William of Orange, a Dutchman and a Protestant, challenged his father-in-law, the Catholic James II, for the British throne. From exile in France, James sailed to Ireland to mobilise allies and met William's army in July 1690 at the River Boyne. The Orangemen, aided by troops from several Protestant countries, vastly outnumbered the Irish and French forces. As battles go, it set no records for scope or tactical innovation. But the anniversary of William's victory is still celebrated with fervour by Protestants in Northern Ireland.

Taoiseach Enda Kenny

sit at Westminster. In 1823 Daniel O'Connell founded the Catholic Association to work for emancipation. Five years later, he won a seat in the House of Commons, but as a Catholic was legally forbidden to take it. To prevent conflict, Parliament passed the Roman Catholic Relief Act (1829), removing the most discriminatory laws and paving the way for Catholic Emancipation.

STARVATION AND EMIGRATION

One of the worst disasters of 19th-century Europe was the Great Famine. The problem emerged in September 1845, when potato blight was found on farms in southeast Ireland. The British government set up an investigation, but the outbreak was misdiagnosed. The next crop failed nationwide, wiping out the staple food of the Irish peasant. Cruel winter weather and the outbreak of disease added to the horror of starvation. Believing that they should not interfere with free market forces, the British government did not provide relief.

Survivors fled the stricken land aboard creaking 'coffin ships'. Irish refugees swamped towns such as Liverpool, Halifax, Boston and New York. The famine reduced the population of Ireland by two million – half dying, the rest emigrating. It took another century for the decline in population figures to be reversed and the flow of emigrants stemmed.

FRUSTRATION AND REVOLT

At the end of the 19th century Nationalist sentiment grew and in 1905 a number of nationalist groups were consolidated in a movement called Sinn Féin ('We Ourselves').

The Easter Rising of 1916 rebels seized the General Post Office in Dublin and declared Ireland's independence from Britain. The authorities crushed the rising, which had lacked support, but their pitiless execution of the ringleaders reversed public opinion. The fight for independence had begun.

At the next general election the nationalist Sinn Féin, led by Eamon de Valera, won by a landslide. The newly elected Sinn Féin parliamentarians refused to take their seats in the Commons in London, but set themselves up in Dublin as Dáil Éireann, the new parliament of Ireland.

More than two years of guerrilla warfare followed until the partition of Ireland was agreed in December 1921. Under it, six counties of the north, where the Protestant majority rejected rule from Dublin, were allowed to remain part of the United Kingdom. The other 26 counties had a Catholic majority and became the Irish Free State (Éire), a dominion within the British Empire. The British hoped that the two sides would soon patch up their differences, but few republicans accepted the settlement and a bitter civil war broke out in the South, lasting until 1923. Nine years later Eamon de Valera came to power, vowing to reinstate the ancient Gaelic language and culture. The 26 counties remained neutral in World War II and formally became an independent republic in 1949.

Britain left Northern Ireland to its own devices and its own government. Many

The Liberator

Daniel O'Connell was one of the first Irish Catholics to qualify as a barrister, and went on to secure the repeal of anti-Catholic legislation in 1829, giving him the name 'the Liberator'.

Catholics did not recognise the province's legitimacy, and many Protestants responded by ensuring that jobs and public housing went mainly to Protestants. In 1969 civil rights marches against these injustices were repressed, unleashing an ugly sectarian conflict that lasted for three decades. The Good Friday Agreement, signed in 1998, established the framework for a self-governing Northern Ireland. In 2005, the IRA declared a permanent ceasefire and decommissioned its weapons preparing the way for the formation of a new government in May 2007.

In 2002, Ireland was one of the first twelve countries to adopt the euro. With the creation of new industries and huge investment in infrastructure, the 'Celtic Tiger' roared. Then, in the wake of the global financial crisis, Ireland entered a severe recession. Unregulated deals between bankers and property developers created a multi-billion euro banking debt. The centre-right Fianna Fail party under Taoiseach Brian Cowen decided that the State would take on the bankers' debts, and imposed a series of swingeing pay cuts and tax hikes all round. The party lost the 2011 election resoundingly, and a coalition government under Enda Kenny assumed power. The historic visit of Her Majesty Queen Elizabeth II in May 2011, in which she laid a wreath in the Garden of Remembrance alongside the then-President Mary McAleese in a widely appreciated gesture of reconciliation, was a beacon of hope in a bleak economic landscape followed by another moment of reconciliation in 2012 when the Queen shook hands with Northern Ireland's deputy first minister Martin McGuinness. In 2012 Ireland was ranked the 7th most developed nation in the world and since 2014, the economic doom of the Great Recession has been averted and the country has experienced strong economic growth.

HISTORICAL LANDMARKS

c.7000 BC Date of earliest archaeological evidence along the coast.

c.500 BC Celts migrate to Britain. Ireland's Iron Age begins.

c.432 St Patrick converts Ireland to Christianity.

1014 Brian Ború, High King of Ireland, defeats Vikings near Clontarf.

1366 Statutes of Kilkenny forbid English to intermarry or speak Gaelic.

1541 Henry VIII declares himself King of Ireland.

1649 Oliver Cromwell conquers Ireland in a merciless campaign.

1690 William of Orange defeats England's Catholic King James II at the Battle of the Boyne.

1800 Act of Union makes Ireland part of the United Kingdom.

1845–51 The Great Potato Famine; over 1 million people die.

1905 Sinn Féin ('We Ourselves') is formed.

1918–23 Sinn Féin wins a landslide of seats in parliament and forms Irish parliament in Dublin. After the 1919–21 Irish War of Independence, the treaty creates the Irish Free State, excluding the six counties of Northern Ireland.

1937 The Free State, Éire, adopts its own constitution.

1949 Having remained neutral in World War II, Éire leaves the British Commonwealth and becomes the Republic of Ireland.

1972 British soldiers shoot dead 13 demonstrators on 'Bloody Sunday'. Belfast's parliament is dissolved. Northern Ireland is ruled from London.

1973 The Republic of Ireland joins the EEC (now the European Union).

1998 The Good Friday Agreement is signed in Northern Ireland.

2002 The Republic of Ireland adopts the euro.

2011 After the collapse of the Fianna Fail government, a coalition government is formed by Fine Gael and Labour. Queen Elizabeth II pays her first visit to Ireland. Michael D. Higgins is elected as Ireland's President.

2012 Northern Ireland's deputy first minister and ex-IRA commander Martin McGuinness shakes hands with Queen Elizabeth II in a historic moment of reconciliation.

2015 The Republic of Ireland legalises same-sex marriage.

WHERE TO GO

The best way to see Ireland is by car, though various package deals or bus tours exist as an alternative. You can see a good deal of the country using public transport, although apart from the main routes, the bus schedules are designed more for locals than tourists.

This book covers the highlights of the Republic and Northern Ireland, starting in Dublin and proceeding clockwise. We cannot describe all the sights – or all the counties – but wherever you go, you'll enjoy Ireland best at an unhurried Irish pace.

DUBLIN

The Republic of Ireland's capital (pop. over 1.8 million) is the birthplace and inspiration of many great authors, and an elegant European city with many outstanding examples of 18th-century architecture. **Dublin ❶** pervaded by contrasting moods; from its noble avenues and intimate side streets to chic shopping and traditional pubs, there are also museums, colleges and plenty of sports. In this melting pot of old and new, traditional lace still masks modern windows.

O'CONNELL STREET TO ST STEPHEN'S GREEN

The main avenue in Dublin is **O'Connell Street**. Measuring 46m (150ft) across, it has five monuments to Irish history lined along the middle. The Millennium Spire, a 395ft high stainless steel monument, replaced the 19th-century Nelson's Pillar blown up by anti-British rebels in 1966.

> **What's in a name?**
>
> The city's name comes from the Irish 'Dubh Linn', meaning 'a dark pool'. The much older Gaelic name, 'Baile Átha Cliath', means 'the town of the hurdle ford'.

The statue of James Joyce off O'Connell Street

O'Connell Street's most famous landmark is the **General Post Office**. The GPO was the command post of the 1916 Easter Rising and was badly damaged in the fighting. A plaque on the front of the building and paintings inside mark the event. There is also the An Post Museum tracing the history of the post office in Ireland.

Just opposite O'Connell Bridge is the imposing monument honouring 'The Liberator', Daniel O'Connell (1775–1847, see page 20), after whom both the street and bridge are named.

From the bridge, wider than it is long, you can look up and down the **River Liffey** and along the embankments. To the east, rises the copper dome of the 18th-century **Custom House**. Like many buildings along the Liffey, it was badly damaged in the civil war of 1921. Further east lies the shiny new IFSC (Irish Financial Services Centre), gateway to the high-rise Docklands area, with modern apartments and the

Dublin's Ha'penny Bridge at night

2,000-seater Grand Canal Theatre. To the west is the **Ha'penny Bridge**, so called because that's what it originally cost to cross it.

The imposing white building facing College Green on the south side of the River Liffey is a branch of the **Bank of Ireland**, originally home of the Irish parliament in the 18th century. The bank moved in when parliament

Fellows Square and the Old Library at Trinity College

was abolished by the Act of Union in 1801 (see page 19).

Behind the railings at the entrance to **Trinity College** Ⓐ are the statues of two famous alumni – philosopher Edmund Burke and playwright Oliver Goldsmith. Founded by Queen Elizabeth I in 1592, Trinity is a timeless enclave of calm and scholarship in the middle of this bustling city. For centuries it was an exclusively Protestant institution, and as recently as 1956 the Catholic church forbade its students to attend Trinity 'under pain of mortal sin'. Today, TCD, as it is called, is integrated. Students lead informative college tours from a desk at the front porch (June–Sept daily, every 30-40 minutes from 9.45am; Oct–May Fri–Mon, times vary).

The campus forms a monument to the good taste of the 18th century, and visitors enjoy cobbled walks among trimmed lawns, fine old trees, statues and stone buildings. You can also enjoy art exhibitions at the Douglas Hyde Gallery, (www.douglashydegallery.com) and the child-friendly Science Gallery (https://dublin.sciencegallery.com).

The greatest treasures are in the vaulted Long Room in the **Old Library** (June–Sept Mon–Sat 9am–6pm, Sun

9.30am–6pm, Oct–May Mon–Sat 9.30am–5pm, Sun noon–4.30pm; www.tcd.ie), where double-decker shelving holds thousands of books published prior to 1800, and priceless early manuscripts are displayed in glass cases. In the adjacent Colonnades Gallery, queues of tourists reverently wait for a look at the **Book of Kells**. This 340-page parchment wonder, handwritten and illustrated by monks during the 9th century, contains a Latin version of the New Testament. The beauty of the script – the illumination (the decoration of initial letters and words) – and the bright abstract designs make this the most wonderful treasure to survive from Ireland's Golden Age. The vellum leaves are turned every day to protect them from light and to give visitors a chance to come back for more.

A left turn on leaving Trinity by the main gate brings you to the entrance of **Grafton Street** 🅑, the main shopping and social artery of the city's southside. More than anywhere else, Grafton Street demonstrates Dublin's knack for seeming to bustle and dawdle at the same time. Buskers entertain passers-by on their way to Brown Thomas, the city's famous high-end department store and other shopping emporiums, such as the stunning Powerscourt Townhouse Centre or the Stephen's Green Shopping Centre at the south end.

Examples of Europe's finest Georgian houses can be seen facing **Merrion Square**. The discreet, smart brick houses have Georgian doorways flanked by tall columns and topped by fanlights. No two are alike. In a complex of formal buildings on the west side of the square stands the city's largest 18th-century mansion, home of the Duke of Leinster. Today **Leinster House** is the seat of the Irish parliament, which consists of the Senate (Seanad Éireann) and the Chamber of Deputies (the Dáil, pronounced 'doyle'); and just north of here on Merrion Square West is the National Gallery.

At the entrance to the **National Gallery** ⓒ (Mon–Sat 9.15am–5.30pm, Thu until 8.30pm, Sun 11am–5.30pm; free; www.nationalgallery.ie; the Milltown and Dargan wings are closed for upgrade until 2016) you will see a statue of George Bernard Shaw, famous and respected Dubliner known locally as a benefactor of the institution. In the gallery, some 2,000 works of art are displayed. Irish artists receive priority, but other nationalities are well represented, such as Dutch, English, Flemish, French, Italian and Spanish masters, including Fra' Angelico, Rubens, Rembrandt, Canaletto, Gainsborough and Goya. Recent additions include a work by Van Gogh and the gallery's first Renoir.

Buskers on Grafton Street

The main entrance to the **National Museum of Archaeology and History** ⓓ (Tue–Sat 10am–5pm, Sun 2–5pm; free; www.museum.ie), a Dublin institution, is reached from Kildare Street. Its collection of Irish antiquities holds several surprises, from old skeletons and tools to exquisite gold ornaments of the Bronze Age. Famous items include the 8th-century Ardagh Chalice, the delicate Tara Brooch from the same era and the 12th-century Shrine of St Patrick's Bell. You can also see ancient Ogham stones and replicas of the greatest carved stone crosses from the early centuries of Christian Ireland.

Dublin is well-endowed with squares and parks, including **St Stephen's Green** Ⓔ one of the biggest city squares in Europe. During the 18th century the square was almost completely surrounded by elegant town houses. Some survive today, though many conservationists despair at the rapidly declining number. Inside the square is a delightful park with flower gardens and an artificial lake favoured by waterfowl. Among many sculptures and monuments is a memorial to the poet and playwright W.B. Yeats by Henry Moore. Nearby is a bust to commemorate Yeats's friend, Countess Constance Markievicz, who defended the square during the 1916 insurrection, and who was the first woman elected to the British House of Commons (although she declined to take her seat, preferring the Dáil).

Another statue honours the man who paid for landscaping the square: Lord Ardilaun, son of the founder of the Guinness brewery. Some thirsty sightseers might be inspired to find a nearby pub and raise a toast to the stout-hearted benefactor.

MEDIEVAL DUBLIN

Dublin Castle Ⓕ (Mon–Sat 10am–4.45pm, Sun noon–4.45pm; www.dublincastle.ie) was begun in the 13th century, set on a hill above the original Viking settlement on the south bank of the River Liffey, but was mostly rebuilt during the 18th century. Over the years it has served as a seat of government, a prison, a courthouse, and occasionally as a fortress under siege. Many visiting heads of state have stayed in the lavish State Apartments.

Just behind the castle is the **Chester Beatty Library** Ⓖ (Mon–Fri 10am–5pm, Sat 11am–5pm, Sun 1–5pm; closed Mon Nov–Feb; free; www.cbl.ie), a collection of priceless manuscripts and miniatures: jade books from China, early Arabic tomes on geography and astronomy, a sampling of Korans, and rare Gospel texts. Around the corner from the castle stands **City Hall**, built in the late 18th century in solid, classical style. Downstairs, an exhibition tells the story of the Irish capital.

Dublin has two noteworthy cathedrals, and although it is the official capital of what is a predominantly Catholic country, both belong to the Protestant Church of Ireland.

Christ Church Cathedral (Mar and Oct Mon–Sat 9am–6pm, Sun 12.30–2.30pm, 4.30–6pm; Apr–Sept Mon–Sat 9am–7pm, Sun 12.30–2.30pm, 4.30–7pm; Nov–Feb Mon–Sat 9am–5pm, Sun 12.30–2.30pm; www.christchurchdublin.ie) is the older of the two, dating from 1038. One unusual architectural touch is the covered pedestrian bridge over Winetavern Street, which links the church and its Synod Hall. This was built during the Victorian era, but doesn't spoil the overall mood. Otherwise, the cathedral contains Romanesque as well as Early English and fine neo-Gothic elements.

Christ Church Cathedral

The Oliver St John Gogarty Bar in Temple Bar

The crypt, now displaying many of Christ Church's valuable treasures, runs under the length of the church, and is a surviving remnant from the 12th century, during which time the cathedral was expanded by Strongbow (see page 17), whose remains lie buried here. Although regarded as authentic for many decades, modern scholars are in heated debate about the authenticity of the Strongbow tomb. You can see the fine statue of a recumbent cross-legged knight in full armour upstairs.

If you would like to delve deeper into Viking and medieval Dublin visit the Synod Hall to see an impressive living history museum **Dublinia** (Mar–Sept daily 10am–6.30pm; Oct–Feb daily 10am–5.30pm; www.dublinia.ie). Actors recreate how Viking and medieval Dubliners lived and encourage visitors to get involved too. Great for kids of all ages.

A short walk south from Christ Church Cathedral leads to Dublin's newer and larger cathedral, **St Patrick's ❶** (Mar–Oct Mon–Fri 9.30am–5pm, Sat 9am–6pm, Sun 9–10.30am, 12.30–2.30pm, 4.30–6pm; Nov–Feb Mon–Fri 9.30am–5pm, Sat

9am–5pm; Sun 9–10.30am, 12.30–2.30pm; www.stpatricks cathedral.ie), which is dedicated to Ireland's national saint. It is said that St Patrick himself baptised 5th-century converts at a well on this very site; indeed, a stone slab used for covering the well can be found in the northwest of the cathedral. This church was consecrated in 1192, but the present structure dates mostly from the 13th and 14th centuries. The cathedral is known for its association with Jonathan Swift, author of *Gulliver's Travels*, who was appointed dean in 1713 and served until his death in 1745. Many Swiftian relics can be seen in a corner of the north transept, and a simple brass plate in the floor near the entrance marks his grave. Next to this you can see the tomb of the mysterious Stella, one of the two great loves of his life. Above the lintel of the robing room you can read his own bitter epitaph, written in Latin: 'Savage indignation can no longer gnaw his heart. Go, traveller, and imitate, if you can,

TEMPLE BAR

Temple Bar is a network of small streets full of studios, galleries, second-hand bookshops, clothing outlets and music stores. There are countless restaurants, pubs and crafts shops. Many Dubliners regard it as a tourist trap, but it has some worthwhile cultural centres.

Project Arts Centre: theatre and avant-garde art gallery

The Button Factory: nightclub and concert venue.

Irish Film Institute: arthouse cinema with bookshop, café/restaurant, bar and film archive.

Gallery of Photography: exhibits Irish and international work.

National Photographic Archive: maintains and exhibits historical images of Ireland.

Jam Art Factory: Irish art and design shop.

The Ark: arts and entertainment centre for children.

The Four Courts

this earnest and dedicated defender of liberty'.

The talented choirboys of St Patrick's Cathedral sing at the services given every day of the week except Saturdays. A joint choir formed from both cathedrals was the first to sing Handel's *Messiah* when the composer was in Dublin in 1742. A copy from the year 1799 can be seen in **Marsh's Library** (Mon, Wed–Fri 9.30am–5pm, Sat 10am–5pm; www.marsh library.ie), Ireland's first public library, founded in 1701.

Called the 'Left Bank' by tourist officials, **Temple Bar** (see page 33) is Dublin's cultural quarter, running from Westmoreland Street to Christ Church Cathedral. With its 18th- and 19th-century architecture it's not just the cultural quarter of Dublin, but also a land of themed bars and raucous nightclubs. It's at its best on Saturdays with a gourmet food market on Meeting House Square, a book market on Temple Bar Square and a craft and design market on Cow's Lane.

THE NORTH BANK

The most impressive building located on the north bank of the Liffey is the domed home of the **Four Courts** (originally the Chancery, Common Pleas, Exchequer and King's Bench). This is the magnificent work of James Gandon, the respected 18th-century English-born architect who also designed Dublin's Custom

House. The courthouse was seriously damaged by prolonged shelling during the 1922 civil war. After lengthy reconstruction, however, it was restored, and justice continues to be dispensed in the Four Courts.

St Michan's Church (Mar–Oct Mon–Fri 10am–12.45pm and 2–4.30pm, Sat 10am–12.45pm; Nov–Mar Mon–Fri 12.30–3.30pm, Sat 10am–12.45pm; charge for tours of the crypt) just around the corner in Church Street, was founded in 1095 but has been rebuilt several times. Among the curiosities is an unusual 'Penitent's Pew', in which sinners had to sit and confess their sins aloud to the whole congregation. In the crypt, wood coffins and mummies can be seen in a remarkable state of preservation. Some of them have been here for about 800 years, saved from deterioration by the dry atmosphere. You can touch the finger of the mummified crusader for good luck.

The last imposing official building to be designed by the architect James Gandon was the **King's Inns ❶**, which houses the headquarters of the Irish legal profession. It contains an important law library and a magnificent dining hall, where grand portraits of many judges decorate the walls.

On the north side of Parnell Square is Charlemont House, an attractive 18th-century mansion which is now the **Dublin City Gallery The Hugh Lane Ⓜ** (Tue–Thu 10am–6pm, Fri–Sat 10am–5pm, Sun 11am–5pm; free; www.hughlane.ie). It includes works from the fine collection of Sir Hugh Lane, whose drowning in the *Lusitania* disaster of 1915 (see page 59) provoked a long legal battle over custody of his paintings. The current agreement assures the Dublin City Gallery three-quarters of the contested legacy, including works by Corot, Courbet, Manet, Monet and Rousseau. The gallery also houses the Francis Bacon Studio, its contents transported from London in 1998 and meticulously recreated, along with displays of the famous artist's works.

Next door to the gallery, **The Dublin Writers Museum** (daily 9.45am–4.45pm, on some holidays 11am–4.45pm; www.writersmuseum.com) displays photographs, manuscripts and first editions relating to writers such as Swift, Shaw, Yeats, O'Casey, Joyce, Beckett and Behan. At 35 North Great George's Street is the **James Joyce Centre** (Mon–Sat 10am–5pm, Sun noon–5pm, Oct–Mar closed Mon; www.james joyce.ie) for Joyce enthusiasts.

BEYOND THE CENTRE

Phoenix Park (www.phoenixpark.ie) provides Dubliners with nearly 3 sq miles (8 sq km) of beautiful parkland. The perfect way to get around the park is to hire bikes at the main Parkgate St entrance (Tel. 087 379 9946; www.phoenix parkbikes.com). Whizz past Europe's tallest obelisk the Wellington Testimonial and the residence of the President of Ireland *Áras an Uachtaráin* (guided tours Sat only; tel: 01 6770095). Farmleigh House (daily 10am–5pm; www.farm leigh.ie) is a 78-acre (31 hectare) estate with stately home and beautiful gardens that once belonged to the Guinness family. To find out more about the history of the park visit the Phoenix Park Visitor Cemtre and Ashtown Castle (tel: 01 677 0095; Apr–Dec daily 10am–6pm, Jan–Mar Wed–Sat 10am–6pm). On the northeast side of the park, Dublin **Zoo** (www.dublin zoo.ie) provides education and diversion; it is noted for breeding lion cubs in captivity and is one of Europe's oldest zoos (1831).

Evening in Phoenix Park

Malahide Castle

In Kilmainham, a stone tower gate guards the grounds of the **Royal Hospital**, which was a home for army pensioners. Now it is the **Irish Museum of Modern Art** (Tue–Fri 11.30am–5.30pm, Sat 10am–5.30pm, Sun noon–5.30pm; free; www.imma.ie) and holds first-class temporary exhibitions.

The forbidding **Kilmainham Gaol** (Apr–Sept daily 9.30am–6pm; Oct–Mar Mon–Sat 9.30am–5.30pm, Sun 10am–6pm; www.heritageireland.ie) has been carefully restored. Many heroes of Irish nationalism lived and died as prisoners here. The central cellblock shows exhibits from Ireland's stormy history.

Many make their way to the city's biggest commercial enterprise, the **Guinness Brewery**, situated at St James' Gate since 1759. Its dark, full-bodied stout is world-renowned. Visitors to its award-winning **Storehouse** (daily 9.30am–5pm, until 6pm July–Aug; www.guinness-storehouse.com) get an entertaining explanation of how the brew is made and a sample of the finished product.

DUBLIN DAYTRIPS

NORTH OF DUBLIN

In the northeastern part of the Bay, **Howth peninsula** makes an appealing starting point for those wishing to venture out of Dublin. From the vantage point of the 170-m (560-ft) Hill of Howth, you can survey the bay and the sea. Howth Harbour, on the north side of the peninsula, is a fishing port and haven for pleasure boats. From here you can see and visit Ireland's Eye (www.islandferries.net), an islet 1.5km (1 mile) offshore that is popular with birds and bird-watchers.

An early Christian high cross at Monasterboice

Malahide a small resort town, is best known for its **castle** (daily 9.30am–5.30pm; www.malahidecastleand gardens.ie), a two-turreted medieval pile. The spirit of the Talbot family, who resided here for 791 years, still pervades, and is explained by an interpretive centre. Part of the National Portrait Collection is housed here and the castle's rooms are fully furnished, and include a medieval great hall. The Talbot Botanic Gardens were started in 1948, and contain 5,000 labelled species on 250 acres, and seven glass-houses. It is the most important botanic collection after London's Kew Gardens.

Drogheda ❷, a small industrial town, straddles the River Boyne near the site of the 1690 battle in which King James II failed to recover the English crown (see page 19). This medieval city was surrounded by a wall with 10 gates – you can still drive through the 13th-century **St Lawrence's Gate**, with its two towers. In the town centre **St Peter's Church** has been

Winter lottery

The overwhelming demand to see Newgrange during the winter solstice has forced Irish Heritage to hold a lottery. Visitors can sign up in the welcome centre. Or you can email your postal address and contact phone number to brunaboinne@opw.ie and they'll enter your name. From an average 35,000 entries, 50 names are chosen.

dedicated to St Oliver Plunkett (1628–81), the Archbishop of Armagh who was executed by the British for an alleged papist plot. Several relics of the local saint are displayed in the church, including the actual door of his cell at Newgate Prison and, most amazing of all, his head, which is embalmed and kept in a gold case in a side altar.

About 10km (6 miles) to the northwest is **Monasterboice** (St Buite's Abbey), one of Ireland's numerous ancient monastic settlements. Over it stands the jagged top of what is thought to have been the tallest round tower in Ireland, 34m (110ft) high. Along with the remains of two ruined churches there are three important examples of early Christian high crosses, with intricately carved figures.

A high medieval gatehouse guards the approach to **Old Mellifont Abbey** (June–Aug daily 10am–6pm; www.heritage ireland.ie), Ireland's most important early Cistercian monastery. Among the buildings stand the remains of a large church and the Lavabo, a graceful octagonal building of which only four sides remain. The abbey is set in peaceful and verdant country.

The sacred mound at Newgrange

Newgrange ❸ (Brú na Boinne Visitor Centre; daily Feb–Apr and Oct 9.30am–5.30pm; May and late-Sept 9am–6.30pm; June–early Sept 9am–7pm; Nov–Jan 9am–5pm; www.heritage ireland.ie), a large Neolithic tomb in the Boyne Valley, looks like a man-made hilltop, but is in fact an amazing feat of pre-historic engineering – one of Europe's best examples of a passage-grave. The narrow tunnel leading to the central shrine is positioned to let the sun shine in on the shortest day of the year, 21 December. The 19-m (62-ft) tunnel is just high and wide enough to walk through at a crouch. At its end you can stand in the circular vault and look up at the ceiling to see the remarkable 4,000-year-old technique used in its construction.

Carvings in spiral, circular and diamond designs decorate the stones in the inner sanctum and entrance. Outside, a dozen large, upright stones, about a third the original number, form a protective circle. Access is by guided tour only; numbers are limited, so arrive early (last tours 90 min before closing). There are two more Neolithic tumuli at Knowth and Dowth.

The scribes and artists of the monastery at **Kells** in County Meath, produced the nation's most beautiful book, now on display at Trinity College in Dublin (see page 27). The town of Kells has grown up around the monastic settlement, and there is a fine Celtic cross standing at the main traffic junction. In the churchyard are several other stone crosses and a 30-m (100-ft) high round tower.

As its name indicates, **Trim ❹** is a well-kept, tidy town, but the English name is derived from the Irish *Baile Átha Trium*, which means 'the town of the Elder Tree Ford'. Trim claims it has Ireland's largest medieval **castle** (mid-Feb–Oct daily 10am–6pm; Nov–mid-Feb weekends 9am–5pm; www.heritage ireland.ie), once a Norman stronghold. Vast it is, but time has left only the bare bones. The Dublin Gate in the south once contained a prison. Across the river, the Yellow Steeple was part of an Augustinian abbey established in the 13th century; the tower was blown up to keep it out of Cromwell's hands.

WEST OF DUBLIN

County Kildare has some of the greenest pastures in all of Ireland. It's a great area for sports, and there are plenty of historic sites amid the rolling hills. **Maynooth**, a pleasant town with an historic college and the ruins of a 12th-century castle, was famed in the 19th and 20th century as a training centre for priests. Founded in 1795, **St Patrick's College** was one of the foremost Catholic seminaries in the world. It is now part of the National University of Ireland.

Ruined monastery

The ruins of an ancient monastery are at the southern end of County Kildare, in the village of Castledermot. Two beautifully carved crosses remain near the portal of a church that could be as much as 1,000 years old. The design of this ruin is repeated in a new church just a few yards behind it.

On the edge of Celbridge village, **Castletown House** ❺ (mid-Mar–Oct Tue–Sun 10am–6pm; Nov.–mid-Mar Tue–Sun 10am–4pm West Wing Exhibition space and Courtyard Café only; www.castletownhouse.ie) stands at the end of a long avenue of trees. This vast stately home, in Palladian style, was erected in 1722 for the speaker of the Irish House of Commons, William Conolly, and has been restored and refurnished with 18th-century antiques and paintings. Conolly's widow ordered the construction of a monstrous obelisk 5km (3 miles) from the house. Known as Conolly's Folly, it was erected to provide jobs for local workers suffering from the famine of 1740-1.

The administrative centre of the county, **Naas** (the Irish *Nás na Ríogh*, means 'Assembly Place of the Kings') has an important racecourse. So does nearby Punchestown, but the capital of horse racing and breeding is the **Curragh** ❻, a 2,000 hectare stretch of flat racing turf, grazed by sheep and used for exercise gallops by many training stables. It's a shock to come upon a modern grandstand – site of the Irish Sweeps Derby – in the middle of this vast plain.

Many winners of the biggest races are born near Kildare Town at the **National Stud** Farm (daily Feb–Oct 9am–6pm; www.irishnationalstud.ie). Here thoroughbreds live in a first-class 'horse resort'. Beside the Irish Horse Museum, there is an immaculate **Japanese Garden** – once a bog, now a world of tidy shrubs and trees. There's even a lotus pond, teahouse and red wooden bridge.

The town of **Kildare** is also remembered for the double monastery (monks and nuns) founded there by 5th-century St Brigid. Though Vikings and other invaders damaged the buildings quite badly, the shape of the 19th-century **cathedral** features 13th-century elements. Nearby is an ancient round tower still in very good shape, with stairs all the way to the top. Another attraction is Kildare Village (daily 10am–7pm;

www.kildarevillage.com) for chic outlet shopping.

SOUTH OF DUBLIN

Dún Laoghaire ❼ (pronounced Dunleary), just south of Dublin, is Ireland's leading yachting centre with several clubs. The piers at the harbour are 2km (1 mile) long, leaving plenty of space between for the huge fleet of pleasure boats that dock here. Construction of the harbour was a great feat of 19th-century engineering – and is still impressive. The newest addition to the Dun Laoghaire skyline is the ship prow-like

Powerscourt Waterfall

Lexicon Library and Cultural Centre (http://libraries.dlrcoco.ie) with fine views of Dublin Bay from the top floor and a few short steps from the National Maritime Museum (daily 11am–5pm; www.mariner.ie).

Around 1.5km (1 mile) south at **Sandycove** is an 18th-century tower. James Joyce lived in it, and used this experience in the opening of *Ulysses*. The Martello Tower was part of the coastal defences built to keep Napoleon at bay. It is now the **James Joyce Tower and Museum** (daily 10am–6pm, Nov–Mar 10am–4pm; free; www.jamesjoycetower.com). A second Martello Tower can be seen on Dalkey Island (boat trips daily www.kentheferryman.com).

Just across the border in County Wicklow, the Garden of Ireland, the popular resort of **Bray** (www.bray.ie) has a 2-km

(1-mile) sand-and-shingle beach backed by an esplanade. The 7km-Cliff Walk along the Bray Head headland leads to Greystones, a postcard-pretty coastal town.

West of Bray, near Enniskerry, is the grand estate of **Powerscourt** ❽ (daily 9.30am–5.30pm or dusk in winter; www.powers court.ie). Covering 20 hectares (47 acres) of glorious country-side and gardens, the estate has an 18th-century, 100-room mansion at its centre, which was damaged in a fire in 1974. Today it contains an exhibition devoted to the history of the estate. From the house, disciplined terraces descend to a lake with a fountain in the middle. The garden centre is also worth a visit, as is the Powerscourt Waterfall, 5km (3 miles) south of the house. There is an Avoca café for a quick bite to eat.

In a narrow, wooded valley with two lakes stand the evocative ruins of the ancient monastic settlement of **Glendalough** ❾ (mid-Mar–mid-Oct 9.30am–6pm; mid-Oct–mid-Mar 9.30am–5pm; www.glendalough.ie). The hermit St Kevin founded the monas-tery here in the 6th century, evidently inspired by the breath-taking, remote scenery. He planned it as a small, contemplative institution, but as its fame spread far and wide, Glendalough of the Seven Churches became an important monastic centre, until 1398, when it was destroyed by Anglo-Normans.

THE WICKLOW WAY

You'll need the better part of a week to see all of this ancient path, which stretches 132km (82 miles) from the suburbs of Dublin to the Wexford border town of Clonegal. A shorter option is the popular stretch from Knockree, 5km (3 miles) west of Enniskerry, to Glen-dalough. It'll take you about three days to cover this area, and you'll be able to step foot on the highest point of the trail – White Hill, from which on a clear day you can see the mountains in Wales.

The buildings which survive date from the 8th and 12th centuries. The most famous is the **round tower**, which is 34m (112ft) high and 16m (52ft) in circumference at the base. This was the place to sit out any sieges; its doorway is built 3.5m (11ft) above the ground – enough to discourage even Vikings from invading. Remnants of a cathedral, stone churches and decorated crosses can also be seen, and the original gateway to the settlement, the only one of its kind in Ireland, is still standing. Inside, on the right, a cross-inscribed stone may

In the Irish National Heritage Park

have marked the limit of the sanctuary granted to those who took refuge within the monastery. In the graveyard, tombstones dating back hundreds of years sit next to more recent graves.

In **Avondale,** you can visit **Avondale House and Gardens** (Easter–Oct Tue–Sun 11am–4pm; hours vary; www.heritage island.com), the home of the great 19th-century Irish leader Charles Stewart Parnell. The Georgian house is set in 202 hectares (500 acres) of forest park, making it an ideal destination for walkers. **Russborough House** (daily Mar and Oct–Dec 10am–5pm; May–Sept 10am–6pm; www.russboroughhouse.ie), near Blessington, is an 18th-century Palladian mansion, reputed to be the longest house in Ireland at 210 m (700ft). It houses a wonderful collection of art and antiques, including works by Goya, Gainsborough and Reynolds. The magnificent views across the

Mudflat harbour

In the 9th century Wexford was called *Waesfjord*, meaning 'the harbour of the mudflats'. At low tide, when the bay empties like a sink, the original name still seems appropriate.

ornamental lake towards the Wicklow Mountains are among the best in Ireland.

THE SOUTHEAST

Over the whole year, the southeast enjoys up to an hour more sunshine a day than other parts of Ireland. The better to see – and enjoy – the varied mountains and pastures, rivers, beautiful beaches and delightful old towns.

Enniscorthy (the Irish *Inis Coirthe* means Rock Island) is a colourful inland port on the River Slaney, navigable from here to Wexford. High above the steep streets of the town, Vinegar Hill is a good vantage point for viewing the country-side. It was the scene of the last battle of the 1798 United Irishmen Rebellion, during which British General Lake over-whelmed the Wexford rebels armed with pitchforks and pikes. **Enniscorthy Castle** (Apr–Sept Mon–Fri 9.30am–5pm, Sat–Sun noon–5pm, Oct–Mar Mon–Fri 10am–4pm, Sat–Sun noon–5pm; www.enniscorthycastle.ie), in the centre of town, is an imposing Norman keep, rebuilt during the 16th century. It reopened in 2011 after a major renovation, and is benefit-ting from its resemblance to Harry Potter's school, Hogwarts.

WEXFORD

Wexford, the county seat, 24km (15 miles) south of Ennis-corthy, was one of the first Viking settlements. A few ancient monuments survive and are well signposted, with informative plaques explaining local legends.

The **Irish National Heritage Park** ❿ (daily 9.30am–6.30pm, until 5.30pm in Sept–Apr; www.inhp.com) in Ferrycarrig, north of the town, contains a collection of life-size replicas of ancient

dwellings, burial sites, old monastic settlements and fortifications, from early Irish man to the 12th century. The Irish
Agricultural Museum and Johnstown Castle Gardens (Mar–
May Mon–Fri 9am–5pm, Sat–Sun 11am–5pm, Jun–Aug 9am–
6.30pm, Sat–Sun 11am–6.30pm, Nov–Feb 9am–4pm, Sat–Sun
11am–4pm www.irishagrimuseum.ie) is a magnificent spot for
a picnic in the lakeside gardens, designed by Daniel Robertson
who also designed Powerscourt Gardens in Co Wicklow.

In October, the Wexford Opera Festival (www.wexfordopera.
com) attracts world performers and fans for little-known
works. Southeast of the town, the resort of **Rosslare** has a
10-km (6-mile) crescent of beach. At Rosslare Harbour, car
ferries arrive from and depart
for Fishguard, Pembroke,
Roscoff and Cherbourg.

Waterford crystal in the making

The tip of the **Hook peninsula** has the 700-year-old
Hook Lighthouse (http://hook
heritage.ie) whose light has
been kept burning at Hook
Head for the past 1,500 years.
For fans of the supernatural,
a visit to Loftus Hall (http://
loftushall.ie), Ireland's most
haunted house, is a must-do.

The Norse established ports
in Dublin and Wexford, but
it somehow never occurred
to them to found permanent
settlements inland. It was the
Normans who moved 32km
(20 miles) up the estuary to
build **New Ross** ⓫, a sizeable

town and still an important inland port. By the riverbank you will see the tall masts of the Dunbrody Famine Ship (daily 9–6pm, Oct–Mar 5pm; www.dunbrody.com), a full scale replica of a sailing ship built in 1845 to transport emigrants to North America.

The isolated hamlet of **Dunganstown**, near New Ross, was the birthplace of US President John F. Kennedy's great grandfather. The Kennedy Homestead (www.kennedyhomestead.ie) is a unique cultural museum showcasing the history of the Kennedy family. The assassinated president was much admired in Ireland and a group of Irish-Americans and the Irish government later created the **John F. Kennedy Arboretum**, above Dunganstown.

WATERFORD

Waterford ⑫ is a largely Georgian port 29km (18 miles) from the open sea. From the far side of the River Suir, its long quayside presents a pretty image. Founded in the 9th century, the town did not gain a charter until 1205, granted by King John. The heritage centre has ancient relics from the Norse and Norman settlements and audiovisual displays. Municipal mementos, including Waterford's important collection of medieval charters, are preserved inside **Reginald's Tower**, the city's most venerable building (mid-Mar–Dec daily 9.30am–5.30pm, Jan–early Mar Wed–Sun 9.30am–5pm). The walls of this giant circular fortification, 3m (10ft) thick and about 24m (80ft) tall, have survived many sieges since being erected in 1003.

Among other attractions are the Garter Lane Arts Centre (www.garterlane.ie), a lively venue in a converted town house; the Mall, an elegant Georgian street beginning at the Quay; and Waterford City Hall, built in the 1780s, which has many fine features, including two small theatres and a Council Chamber illuminated by a splendid chandelier made from the famous **Waterford crystal**.

Cahir Castle

The golden age of Waterford crystal ran from 1783 to 1851. After a century's lapse, production resumed, only to cease again in 2009. The skills of lowing and cutting lead crystal continue to be demonstrated in the **Waterford Crystal Visitor Centre on the Mall** (factory tour Jan–Feb and Nov–Dec Mon–Fri 9.30am–3.15pm; Mar Mon–Sat 9am–3.15pm, Sun 9.30am–3.15pm; Apr–Oct Mon–Sat 9am–4.15pm, Sun 9.30am–4.15pm; www.waterford visitorcentre.com).

In **Lismore** ⓭ at the western edge of the county, the **Lismore Experience**, another educational multimedia show, tells the history of this small town founded in the 7th century by St Carthage. Also, **Ormond Castle** in Carrick-on-Suir, Co Tipperary is the finest Elizabethan manor house in Ireland, now restored to its 16th-century glory.

Counties **Kilkenny** and **Tipperary** both feature stunning scenery and imposing ruins. Tipperary was home of the kings of Munster; Kilkenny entered history as the ancient Kingdom of Ossory. The main town in County Tipperary is **Clonmel**, where parts of the 14th-century walls can still be seen. The turreted West Gate was rebuilt in 1831 on the site of an original gate. Tipperary County Museum (Tue–Sat 10am–4.45pm) on Mick Delahunty Square is well worth a visit.

The name of the town of **Cahir** is a short version of the Irish for 'Fortress of the Dun Abounding in Fish'. Its setting, on the River Suir, is both attractive and strategic. The seemingly impregnable **Cahir Castle** (daily Mar–mid-June 9.30am–5.30pm; mid-June–Aug 9am–6.30pm; Sept–mid-Oct 9.30am–5.30pm; mid-Oct–Feb 9.30am–4.30pm; www.heritageireland.ie) guards the crucial crossing. Built on the river's lovely islet – a site fortified since the 3rd century – the present castle dates from the 15th century. It's in a fine state of restoration, and guided tours point out military details, such as musket slits, a portcullis and a cannonball embedded high in one of the walls. While you're in Cahir, take a look at **Swiss Cottage** (Apr–Oct daily 10–6pm; www.heritageireland.ie), an early 19th-century romantic cottage, in the bright Regency style. It has been fully restored right down to the thatched roof and original French wallpaper.

CASHEL

In **Cashel**, ⑭ Co Tipperary, monastic ruins crown an imposing hilltop. The **Rock of Cashel** (daily mid-Mar–early June and mid-Sept–mid-Oct 9am–5.30pm; early June–mid-Sept 9am–7pm; mid-Oct–mid-Mar 9am–4.30pm; www.heritageireland.ie), is a 61-m (200-ft) high outcrop of limestone, where the kings of Munster had their headquarters from the 4th to the 12th centuries. St Patrick visited in 450 and baptised King Aengus and his brothers. In 1101 ecclesiastical authorities built an Irish-Romanesque church on it. **Cormac's Chapel** (consecrated in 1134) is unique in that it was built by Irish monks who interpreted architectural styles they had studied in Europe. It features a steeply pitched stone roof, rows of blank arches and two oddly positioned towers. Stone-carvings of beasts and abstract designs decorate the doorway and arches.

The chapel is dwarfed by the **cathedral** which abuts it. This structure, dating from the 13th century, has thick and well-preserved walls, but the roof collapsed during the 18th century. On the positive side, the resulting hole lets the sunlight stream in, helping to clarify the many architectural details, as well as the exquisite medieval stone-carvings.

Inside the entrance, St Patrick's Cross is one of the oldest crosses in Ireland, and it looks like it – the sculptures on both sides are very weather-beaten. The cross rises up from the 'Coronation Stone', said to have been a pagan sacrificial altar.

It was in the lively market town of **Thurles**, in 1174, that the Irish forces defeated the Anglo-Norman army led by Strongbow (see page 17). Seven hundred years later, the town was to be the birthplace of the Gaelic Athletic Association

Holy Cross Abbey

Old shops line the square in Inistioge, Kilkenny

(GAA), now an amateur sports organisation with 500,000 members world-wide. The Lár na Páirce GAA Museum (Mon–Sat 10am–5.30pm; http://larnapairce.ie) tells the story of Gaelic games. The most conspicuous landmark of the town, the Catholic Cathedral, was built in a 19th-century version of the Romanesque style. The square bell tower, 38m (125ft) high, can be seen for miles around.

On the west bank of the River Suir, 6km (4 miles) south of Thurles is the Cistercian **Holy Cross Abbey**. Construction of the church here, which is still in use, started in Romanesque style, but slowly evolved into Gothic. The solid white walls, enhanced by window-tracery, reach up to a perfectly restored 15th-century ceiling. A triple-arched recess contains seats of honour carved from jet-black marble and decorated with ancient coats of arms. Another detail is the night stairs, down which the monks stumbled from their sleeping quarters at 2am to chant matins. One of the bells in the tower was cast in the early 13th century, making it Ireland's oldest.

KILKENNY

Kilkenny ⑮ has many historic buildings and an attractive town centre, with an enormous medieval castle with acres of lawns smack bang in the centre – and a river to boot. This was the capital of the old Kingdom of Ossory, a small, feuding realm in pre-Norman Ireland. Parliament, which convened here in 1366, passed the notorious but ineffectual Statutes of Kilkenny, with the aim of segregating the Irish from the Anglo-Normans; in those days intermarriage was seen as high treason. In the 17th century an independent Irish parliament met here for several years. Oliver Cromwell took the town for the English in 1650, suffering heavy losses in the process.

The Irish *Cill Choinnigh* means St Canice's church. **St Canice's Cathedral**, built in the 13th century, is on the original site of the church which gave the town its name. Though Cromwell's rampaging troops badly damaged the building, it has since been restored to an admirable state. Alongside it is a round tower.

Kilkenny Castle (daily Mar 9.30am–5pm; Apr–May and Sept 9.30am–5.30pm; June–Aug 9am–5.30pm; Oct–Feb 9.30am–4.30pm; www. kilkennycastle.ie) was built in the 13th century to replace the primitive fortress erected by Strongbow. The Butler family, one of the great Anglo-Norman dynasties, held the castle until 1935, but today it is owned by the Irish state. The ornate Georgian stable of the Castle Yard opposite houses the headquarters of the Design and Crafts Council Ireland (www. dccoi.ie) and the National Craft Gallery (www.national craftgallery.ie). Kilkenny

Kilkenny Castle

St Finbarr's Cathedral in Cork City

was at the forefront of the revival of traditional handicrafts and innovative design in Ireland, and the 'craft trail' (brochures available locally; www.madeinkilkenny.ie) is well worth following.

Kilkenny is packed with bright shops. In the High Street, the Tholsel (city hall), dating from the 18th century, has an eight-sided clock tower. **Rothe House** (http://rothehouse.com), a Tudor town house dating from 1594, now a museum. The exhibits range from Stone Age tools unearthed locally to medieval relics.

Just outside of **Thomastown**, a charming little town with nice pubs and lunch venues, you can visit the partially restored ruins of the Cistercian **Jerpoint Abbey** (daily early Mar–Sept 9am–5.30pm; Oct 9am–5pm; Nov–early Dec 9.30am–4pm; www.heritageireland.ie). Founded in the mid-12th century by the King of Ossory, it had a brief, troubled history before succumbing to the dissolution of the monasteries in 1540. Parts of it retain their Romanesque lines, but the square central tower with its stepped battlements was added during the 15th century. Much of the sculptural work in the cloister and church is intact, and you can see larger-than-life carvings of knights and saints.

From Thomastown, make the journey to the picturesque village of **Inistioge**, just 7km (5 miles) away and the location for a few famous films, most recently *The Secret Scripture* starring Rooney Mara, Vanessa Redgrave, Aidan Turner and Eric Bana. While here, **Woodstock Gardens & Arboretum** are perfect for a scenic woodland walk.

THE SOUTHWEST

CORK

Ireland's largest county marries gently rolling farmland with rugged, stony peninsulas and delightful bays. Enclosed by steep hills, **Cork City ⑯** has all the facilities of an important commercial and industrial centre, but its atmosphere is unique. The River Lee divides into two channels to the west of the city centre, leaving the centre on an island connected to its north and south banks by numerous bridges, with seagulls flying overhead and swans gliding by.

The city's name is an anglicisation of *Corcaigh*, or 'Marshy Place', which is how the area looked in the 6th century when St Finbarr arrived to found a church and school. In the year 820 the Vikings raided marshy Cork, destroying the institutions and houses. They liked the lay of the land and returned to build their own town on the same site. This destruction and rebuilding was repeated in the 17th century and then again during the Irish War of Independence, 1919–21.

The impressive dome of St Finbarr's

The main office for Cork and Kerry Tourism is located on the Grand Parade in Cork and offers free maps of the city centre. Cork's beauty

Cobh Harbour

begs slow exploration and one can easily spend the day strolling along its narrow canals and winding streets.

Patrick Street, fondly known as 'Pana' by locals is the wide main street of Cork. It is curved because it was built above a river channel. It makes for great window-shopping anytime and is full of people promenading on Saturday afternoons. A venture across the south channel of the River Lee will take you to **St Finbarr's Cathedral**. The latest version was built in the 19th century and follows the lofty French-Gothic style, with arches upon arches. Across the river's north channel on the Christy Ring Bridge and up the hill is Shandon Church. This distinctive steeple has always been a favourite city landmark. Visitors can climb up through the clockwork intricacies and even play a tune on the bells.

Nearby, at Sunday's Well you can visit the fully restored 19th/early 20th-century cells of the **Cork City Gaol** (daily Oct–Mar 10am–4pm, Apr–Sept 9.30am–5pm; http://corkcitygaol. com). The same building high above the city was the location of Cork's first radio station which is now a delightfully idiosyncratic radio museum.

COUNTY CORK

Cork is a good centre for excursions. **Blarney Castle** ⓱ (Mon–Sat, May and Sept 9am–6.30pm; June–Aug 9am–7pm; Oct–Apr 9am–sunset or 5.30pm; Sun summer 9.30am–5.30pm, winter 9.30am–sunset; www.blarneycastle.ie) is 8km (5 miles) to the west. The original owner of the castle, the chieftain Cormac MacCarthy, had a habit of employing soothing but evasive chatter (dubbed the 'blarney') as delaying tactics. Today, in order to acquire similar eloquence, tourists climb up to the battlement, lie flat on their backs, hang on to two iron bars and extend the head backwards in order to kiss an awkwardly placed stone. Most visitors play along with this preposterous legend.

The castle itself is worth a visit, even if mighty hordes of tourists do besiege it every summer. The formidable keep was built in the middle of the 15th century, while the private park, in which the castle stands, includes a grove of ancient yew trees, said to be a site of Druid worship.

Cobh ⓲, the seaport of Cork city, lies about 24km (15 miles) east of Cork City. It is pronounced 'Cove', which is exactly what it means in Irish.

From Queen Victoria's visit in 1849, until 1922, Cobh was called Queenstown. The port is touched by nostalgia – from the days of the great transatlantic liners and the earlier, more tragic traffic of desperate emigrants fleeing the Irish famine for Canada or America. **The Queenstown Story** (www.cobhheritage.com) and the Titanic Experience (www.titanicexperiencecobh.ie) provide a particular insight into this era. High above the harbour, the spire of the **Cathedral of St Colman** reaches heavenward. Recitals are given in the summer on the cathedral's 47-bell carillon.

In Midleton, to the northeast of Cobh, visit the **Old Midleton Distillery** (guided tours Apr–Oct daily 10am–4.30pm; Nov–Mar daily at 11.30am, 1.15, 2.30 and 4pm; www.tours.jameson whiskey.com) in a converted whiskey distillery that dates back to the late 18th century. It tells the story of Irish whiskey via an audiovisual presentation, and offers a tour with tastings.

The town of **Youghal** (pronounced 'Yawl'), east of Midleton, is a resort with 8km (5 miles) of beach and a long seafaring history. The town walls from the Middle Ages can still be seen.

On the site of the main town gate is the **clock tower** from 1776. The high street runs right through it with the structure's four narrow floors and belfry rising above an arched platform over the street. The attractive tower was once a prison, and insurrectionists were hanged from the windows to set an example to the populace.

The most impressive monument in Youghal, **St Mary's Collegiate Church** (Church of Ireland), is thought to have been founded in the 5th century. The present building dates largely from the 13th century, and was restored in the 19th. Among the monuments and tombs in the church is one built, in his own honour, by Richard Boyle, an Elizabethan adventurer and the first Earl of Cork. Myrtle Grove, a 16th-century house near the churchyard entrance, was briefly home to Sir Walter Raleigh. The Heritage Centre (www.eastcork tourism.com) on the quayside runs guided tours.

Steep hills shelter the seaport of **Kinsale** ⑲, about 29km (18 miles) south of Cork. Its wide, sheltered harbour is a joy to sailors and sightseers alike. Kinsale

Kinsale besieged

Kinsale was under siege in 1601 as Spanish troops, who had sailed to aid the Irish against Queen Elizabeth, were defeated, sparking the 'flight of the Earls' (the exodus of the Irish nobility) and the redistribution of their lands.

The Old Head of Kinsale

is renowned for its restaurants, which are among the best in southwest Ireland.

Today, the **harbour** is used by fishing boats, dinghies and yachts. Ashore are fortifications including the **Charles Fort** (daily Nov–mid-Mar 10am–5pm; mid-Mar–Oct 10am–6pm; www.heritageireland.ie), the Norman church of St Multose, a museum housing Edward III's first town charter, and the **Desmond Castle International Museum of Wine**.

Migratory birds inhabit the **Old Head** of Kinsale, 16km (10 miles) beyond the town. A modern lighthouse here is the successor to a beacon dating back to pre-Christian times. It was off the Old Head that a German submarine torpedoed the world-famous liner, the *Lusitania*, on 7 May 1915, resulting in the loss of 1,500 lives. The inquest into the disaster was held in the Kinsale Court House.

Clonakilty, another coastal town situated between Kinsale and Bantry, is home to the **West Cork Model Railway Village** (daily 11am–5pm; www.modelvillage.ie) that depicts the area's six towns, with a working model of the defunct West Cork Railway.

The town of **Bantry** nestles between steep green hills and a tranquil bay. The main sight is Bantry House (Apr–Oct daily 10am–5pm; Apr–May and Sept–Oct Mon garden only; www. bantryhouse.com), a part-Georgian, part-Victorian stately home full of tapestries, paintings and furnishings and set in sub-tropical gardens.

Heading counter-clockwise around the bay from Bantry, the highway weaves through more rocky hills until it descends upon **Glengarriff** ⓴, where the beauty of the setting and the pleasant climate account for its year-round popularity.

Boat trips (www.bluepoolferry.com; www.harbourqueenferry. com) touted by traditional boatmen in Glengarriff cruise past Seal Island, and you can opt to land on **Garinish Island** (Apr–Oct daily times vary; www.garnishisland.com) a 15-hectare (37-acre) garden. The flora comes from five continents, and the centre-piece is a walled **Italian garden**, surrounding a pool, with the gentle air of a paradisiacal perfume factory. Until 1910, Garinish was a bleak military outpost. From the top of the Martello tower, sentries once kept a lookout for Napoleonic invasion fleets; today, you can survey the luxuriant hills around the bay.

COUNTY KERRY

By any standard this is a spectacular part of the world: the Atlantic in all its moods, lakes designed for lovers or poets, and steep, evergreen mountains. **Killarney** ㉑ is a good base from which to explore the area. Seeing the sights here can be accomplished in many ways – by car, coach, bicycle, boat or even by 'jaunting car' – a horse-drawn rig driven by a *jarvey* (guide) who knows the territory and how to tell a story.

It is best to visit the **Gap of Dunloe** on an organised excursion, usually a half-day trip. The Gap, a wild gorge 6km (4 miles)

The Ring of Kerry

long, can be traversed on a pony, in a pony trap or on foot. Sound effects underline the weirdness of the eerie rock-strewn scenery as echoes bounce off the mountains – **MacGillycuddy's Reeks** in the west (the highest range in Ireland), and to the east, **Purple Mountain**. The long trek leads to the shore of the Upper Lake, where the tour continues by boat to Ross Castle. The scenery around the lakes – thick forests, stark crags and enchanted islands – could not be more romantic, but there's adventure, too: the **rapids** at Old Weir Bridge.

Muckross Abbey is a friary dating from the 15th century with a massive square tower, a cloister with Gothic arches on two sides, Norman or Romanesque on the others and an old, weathered yew tree. **Muckross House** (daily 9am–5.30pm, until 7pm July and Aug; www.muckross-house.ie), which contains exhibits of Kerry crafts and folklore, is surrounded by outstanding gardens. Muckross Traditional Farms (same hours and website) is an enjoyable outdoor attraction recreating traditional farming methods and way of life in the 1930s.

RING OF KERRY

The **Ring of Kerry** 🕮 may well be the most sensational 180km (112 miles) you have ever driven. The ring is a circular route around a coast of rugged cliffs and the enthralling seascapes. This round-trip can be made in either direction, but here we proceed clockwise. Set aside a whole day to really make the most of it.

Leaving Killarney, the road goes past lush lakeland. **Kenmare** is famous for lacemaking and the fish which fill its estuary. North of the small resort of Castlecove, 3km (2 miles) off the main road, are the ruins of **Staigue Fort**. A 2,500-year-old stronghold and one of Ireland's main archaeological wonders, this almost circular structure measures about 27m (90ft) across with a 6m (18ft) wall.

Near Caherdaniel, **Derrynane House**, the home of Daniel O'Connell (see page 20), has been fully restored and is now a museum (Mar and Oct Wed–Sun 10am–5pm; Apr–Sept daily 10.30am–6pm; Nov–mid-Dec Sat–Sun 10am–4pm; www.heritageireland.ie). Game fishing lures visitors to Waterville, as well as the scenery nearby: stark grey glaciated mountains on one side of the road, green fields and the sea on the other.

Crag Cave

To the east of Tralee, the town of Castleisland is the location of the Crag Cave (daily mid-Mar–Dec, Fri–Sun Jan–mid-Mar). Nearly 4km (2.5 miles) long and bristling with stalagmites and stalactites, this is one of the best show caves in Ireland.

A bridge connects **Valentia Island**, with its high slate cliffs, to the mainland at Portmagee. The island was the European terminus of the first Atlantic cable (1866), making possible the first telegraphic contact with America.

Off Valentia, the Skelligs Islands rise abruptly from

the ocean, shrouded with mystery and birds. Skellig Michael and its monastic ruins are a UNESCO World Heritage Site. Filming for Star Wars took place here in 2014 and 2015. Find out more at the Skelligs Heritage Centre (www.skelligexperience.com) or take a boat to the islands (http://skelligislands.com).

On the north shore of the peninsula, hills plunge to sea level and cliffs complete the descent. **Dingle Bay** seems startlingly wide and the Dingle Peninsula iteslf looks like another country.

Slea Head on the Dingle Peninsula

From Glenbeigh to Killorglin, the head of the bay is almost totally protected from the rough sea by huge sandbars extending from either shore. **Rossbeigh Strand**, with its 6km (4 miles) of golden sand, is a dream beach.

The last town on the ring, **Killorglin**, saves all its energy for three days in August and a boisterous pagan pageant called the Puck Fair (http://puckfair.ie), during which time a mountain goat presides over round-the-clock festivities. To the north, **Tralee** ㉓, the administrative centre of County Kerry, owes its fame to the songwriter William Mulchinock (1820–64). *The Rose of Tralee* and its author are honoured in a monument in the town park. The rose also calls the tune of Tralee's annual festival in late August, when girls of Irish descent from many countries compete in a beauty contest, and the winner is crowned Rose of Tralee (www.roseoftralee.ie).

Kerry County Museum (Jan–May Tue–Sat 9.30am–5pm; June–Aug daily 9.30am–5.30pm; Sept–Dec daily 9.30am–5pm; www.kerrymuseum.ie) in Tralee offers three experiences all in one. Kerry in Colour is an audiovisual presentation of the splendours of Kerry; the County Museum details Kerry's history since 5000 BC; and the Geraldine Experience reconstructs life in medieval Tralee.

Tralee is the principal gateway to the **Dingle Peninsula**, a long, dramatic finger which points some 48km (30 miles) into the Atlantic Ocean. On the south shore, amidst rocky coves, a sandbar grows into an arc of beach jutting more than half-way across the bay. **Inch Strand's** 6km (4 miles) of sand slide gently into the sea. Behind the bathers, archaeologists putter about the dunes, where inhabitants of prehistoric ages left meaningful clues about their way of life.

The small fishing port and resort of **Dingle** ㉔ (officially known as An Daingean, the name to look for on signposts) claims to be the most westerly town in Europe. From here to land's end all the hamlets are Irish-speaking parts of the Gaeltacht (see page 124), where folklore and traditional language are still preserved. This is very harsh farming country, where old stone walls are overrun with shrubs and rugged hedges divide skimpy parcels of land into fields. You'll see the sheep grazing on even the most precipitous of hills.

The western part of the peninsula is rich territory for archaeologists. In one area, the Fahan group alone consists of an astonishing 400 *clocháns* (beehive-shaped stone huts), along with forts and other ancient structures. For a spectacular panorama, drive up the **Conor Pass** (at an altitude of 460m/1,500ft) and see the sea out to the north and south, and mountains and lakes on the east and west sides. In this part of the world you're isolated from everything but the wild fuchsia and heather beside the road.

THE WEST

LIMERICK AND CLARE

By the time the waters of the River Shannon have reached **Limerick** in the west, they have flowed over 274km (170 miles) through thick and thin, from narrow streams and howling rapids to lakes and lochs. After Limerick they still have another 97km (60 miles) to travel through the estuary to the open Atlantic.

Limerick's position at the meeting of the river and its tidal waters assured the city a long and often violent history. The Danes were first on the scene. Their belligerence provoked repeated attacks by the native Irish, who finally drove them out.

King John's Castle in Limerick

The Anglo-Normans in turn captured *Luimneach* – in English 'Bare Spot'. King John visited in 1210 and ordered the construction of a **bridge** and **King John's Castle** (daily 9.30am–5.30pm; www.shannonheritage.com), which still survive and have been extensively renovated. A riverside footpath runs from the Tourist Office on Arthur's Quay to the castle, passing the Hunt Museum and St Mary's Cathedral en route. The city endured its most memorable siege after the Battle of the Boyne (1690), when Irish supporters of James II (see page 19) retired to Limerick pursued by William of Orange. The losers lost again, but the Treaty of Limerick allowed them to leave with honour and guaranteed the Irish freedom of religion. This was repudiated by the English Parliament, so today Limerick carries the title of 'City of the Violated Treaty'.

The extraordinary landscape of the Burren

The 800-year-old **St Mary's Cathedral** (May–Sept Mon–Fri 9am–5pm, Sat 9am–4pm, Sun 10.30am–4pm; Oct–Apr Mon–Fri 9am–5pm, Sat 9am–1pm, Sun 10.30am–1pm; suggested donation) has an arched Irish-Romanesque west door, while 15th-century carved misericords under the choir seats show free-ranging imagination with representations of angels, animals and other figures in relief. The waterfront Custom House is now the Hunt

Museum (Mon–Sat 10am–5pm, Sun 2–5pm; free on Sundays; www.huntmuseum.com), housing an outstanding collection of Celtic and medieval treasures and a selection of 20th-century Irish and European art, including works by Picasso and Renoir.

Barren Burren

A frustrated general serving Oliver Cromwell famously condemned the desolate Burren as having 'not enough wood to hang a man, not enough water to drown him, not enough clay to cover his corpse'.

Shannon Airport reinforces Limerick's historic role as a centre of commerce. It opened in 1945, making its mark before fast, non-stop transatlantic travel became common. Waiting passengers were offered the chance to buy luxury goods exempt from tax. Thus the world's first duty-free shop grew into a shopping centre.

Bunratty Castle ㉖ (daily, 9am–5.30pm; www.shannonheritage.com) is a busy tourist attraction about 5km (3 miles) from the airport. At night actors in period costume recreate medieval banquets for visitors.

A favourite attraction at Bunratty is the **Folk Park** (same hours as the castle) containing replicas of typical old houses of the Shannon region. The peat fires are kept burning, as if the people had just stepped out to milk a cow or catch a fish.

Ennis, the county town of county Clare, has a 13th-century friary, which in the Middle Ages had 350 friars and 600 students. The buildings were expanded over the years, and fully renovated in the 1950s.

THE BURREN

Northwest of Ennis, around 520 sq km (200 sq miles) of County Clare belongs to **the Burren** ㉗. Glaciers and ages of erosion have created limestone pavements – horizontal slabs divided by fissures, like the aftermath of an earthquake. Though

The tribes of Galway

The surnames of the 14 families or 'tribes' of Welsh and Norman descent who controlled medieval Galway are still commonly found in the city: Blake, Bodkin, Browne, D'Arcy, Ffrench, Kirwan, Joyce, Lynch, Morris, Martin, Skerrett, Athy, Dean and Ffont.

sometimes described as a moonscape, the Burren is anything but barren; it is a quiet world of small animals, birds, butterflies and alpine and Mediterranean flowers. It may seem hostile to human habitation, but the profusion of forts and tombs proves it supported a population for several centuries.

Geologists, botanists and archaeologists have field trips on the pavements, and speleologists enjoy the caves. More than 40km (25 miles) of caves have been fully explored. Most are for experts only, but anyone can visit **Aillwee Cave**, southeast of Ballyvaughan (daily Nov–Feb 10am–5pm; Mar–June and Sept–Oct 10am–5.30pm; July–Aug 10am–6.30pm by appointment only in Dec; www.aillweecave.ie). Kilfenora (www.kilfenoraclare.com) is famous for traditional Irish music. The **Burren Centre** (www.theburrencentre.ie) is a pleasant way to get your bearings. The 12th century Kilfenora Cathedral is noted for its sculptured monuments and high crosses.

The **Cliffs of Moher ㉘**, 10km (6 miles) northwest of Lahinch, tower 215m (700ft) over the Atlantic Ocean. From **O'Brien's Tower** (daily, hours vary; www.cliffsofmoher.ie/plan-your-visit), an outpost near to the edge, the cliff faces stand above the sea in horizontal layers as easily defined as the storeys of a glass skyscraper. Huge waves crash against the foot of the cliff but the thump is heard late, like the report of a distant artillery shell. The cliffs are populated by thousands of seabirds.

The town of **Lisdoonvarna** was once famous as a spa. Today it is chiefly known for its Matchmaking Festival (www.matchmakerireland.com) in September after the harvest, when farmers traditionally took a break from farming to seek a wife. The festival is a light-hearted affair, attracting some 40,000 hopeful visitors annually.

Across the border in County Galway, the area around Gort has a number of literary associations. Lady Gregory, co-founder of the Abbey Theatre, lived in **Coole Park**, now a nature reserve (all year; free) with a visitor centre (daily Apr–May and Sept 10am–5pm; June–Aug 10am–6pm; free; www.coolepark.ie). The unique 'autograph tree' is inscribed with the initials of some of her famous visitors – Augustus John, John Masefield, Sean O'Casey and one of the few who is instantly recognized by his initials: George Bernard Shaw.

GALWAY

A gargoyle on Lynch's Castle in Galway

The main city of the western province of Connaught, **Galway 29** is a port, resort, administrative and cultural centre. In medieval times it prospered as a city-state, but withered in the 17th century after prolonged sieges by the forces of Oliver Cromwell and, four decades later, by William of Orange. Remnants of the old glory still shine in a few corners of the renewed city.

The **Collegiate Church of St Nicholas** was begun by the Anglo-Normans in 1320. Following local tradition, Columbus came to pray here

Derryclare Lake in Connemara

before his voyage to America. Today the area around the church is the venue for a lively Saturday morning food and craft market (http://galwaymarket.com).

During Galway's heyday 14 families, mostly of Welsh and Norman descent, formed a sort of medieval Mafia that controlled the economic and political life of the town. Their common enemy, the O'Flaherty family, inspired the inscription (1549) over the old town gate: 'From the fury of the O'Flaherties, good Lord deliver us'.

Of the tribes in Galway, the Lynch family left the most memories and monuments. **Lynch's Castle**, a town house dating from 1600, is decorated with excellent stonework, gargoyles and carved window frames. This rare building has been restored and now houses a bank.

Another reminder of the Lynches is the Lynch Memorial Window in Market St, with a plaque recounting the macabre story of James Lynch Fitzstephen – Mayor of Galway in 1493 – who condemned and executed his own son, Walter, for murder. Judge Lynch had to be the hangman because nobody else would agree to carry out the sentence.

Galway's Catholic cathedral – whose full name is **Cathedral of Our Lady Assumed into Heaven and St Nicholas** – (daily 8.30–6.30pm, www.galwaycathedral.ie) has a giant dome looming over the city. The classical architecture is mislead-ing; the church was dedicated in 1965. Alongside the cathe-dral is Galway's **Salmon Weir**, in which salmon fight their way from the sea up to Lough Corrib. From June to July you can see them queueing up for a chance to leap up the falls and follow their instincts to sweet water.

Galway's seaside suburb, **Salthill**, is a traditional seaside resort with a long promenade and a clean sandy beach. It's a great place to watch the sun set on Galway Bay; sprawling hills enclose most of the bay, but the Atlantic can be seen to the west.

CONNEMARA

Lough Corrib, a loch extending 43km (27 miles) north from Galway, is big enough to be whipped by waves when the wind hurtles down the hillside. It's generally shallow and well sup-plied with islands and fish – salmon, trout, pike and perch. Lough Corrib divides County Galway into two contrasting regions: a fertile limestone plain to the east, and Connemara – a range of dramatic mountains and sparkling lakes – to the west, all enclosed by the coastline of rugged cliffs and pris-tine beaches.

Much of the south coast of Connemara is an Irish-speaking enclave. This is also the home of the Connemara pony – robust, intelligent and self-reliant. Spanish horses of the 16th century are rumoured to have crossbred with Irish ponies; one version says that the stallions swam ashore from ships of the Spanish Armada wrecked across nearby rocks.

The sky seems to change by the minute in the far west

Twelve Bens

The huge Twelve Bens of Connemara ('ben' is Gaelic for peak) constitute a range of moody mountains mostly inhabited by sheep; the foothills are interspersed with bogs and pretty lakes.

An aerial view of Inishmore

– dazzling sun, fleeting clouds and rain alternating so quickly that photographers have to be constantly at the ready. The capital is the well-placed market town of **Clifden** ㉚, a base for exploring the nearby lakes and rivers, as well as fine beaches, bogs and mountains. The town's Irish name is *An Clochán*, meaning 'Stepping Stones'. There are so many areas of water around Clifden that you can't tell the genuine sea inlets from the coves of the lakes, except for the seaweed, a plant which features in Irish cooking more than you'd expect. Nearby is **Kylemore Abbey** (daily mid–Mar–Nov 9.30am–5.30pm, July–Aug until 7pm; Nov–Mar 10am–4.30pm; visitor centre free, gardens and abbey charge; www.kylemoreabbeytourism.ie), the home of Ireland's Benedictine nuns and one of the most photographed buildings in the country.

ARAN ISLANDS

Out in the Atlantic, 48km (30 miles) off Galway, the **Aran Islands** ㉛ are a remote outpost indeed, little more than stone outcrops. In the past islanders had to struggle to survive, cultivating the bleak limestone terrain, which had so little topsoil that they would ship it in from the mainland or scrape it from the cracks between the rocks and mix it with seaweed fertiliser to grow feed for their livestock. Tourism has now improved their fortunes, and though their famous Aran sweaters are still made here, these days few of them are hand-knitted. All the locals speak Gaelic in their daily life, but can also speak English.

Inishmore, 'the Big Island', is 14km (9 miles) from tip to tip and only 3km (2 miles) across. From the air – and you can fly there from Galway (www.aerarannislands.ie) – you can make out tapestries of tiny fields enclosed by dry-stone walls. **Kilronan**, has a port where ferries from the mainland dock. The fishermen work aboard modern trawlers, but the traditional *currachs*, tar-coated boats with canvas hulls, are still used. This is an island to explore on foot or rented bicycle, available at the pier. If you're in a hurry, you can hire pony traps for guided tours, or the island even has a single motorised taxi which doubles as a school bus.

The remarkable monument of **Dún Aengus** (daily Mar 9.30am–4pm; end Mar–Oct 9.45am–6pm; Nov–Dec 9.30am–4pm; Jan–Feb Wed–Sun 9.30am–4pm), a giant prehistoric fortress on the sheer edge of a cliff some 91m (300ft) high, is about a 15-minute walk across the fields from the road. Three layers of stone walls, the outermost 6m (20ft) high, surround the courtyard 46m (150ft) across. With the ramparts and obstacles set up beyond the wall, the total area covers 4 hectares (11 acres). Even in modern times it would take a rash general to stage an attack on Dún Aengus.

Elsewhere on the islands, among colourful wild flowers, grazing cows, sheep and an abundance of bounding rabbits, there are numerous **archaeological sites** of less importance,

Croagh Patrick

that nevertheless have their own diversion to offer. Here you'll find stone forts and groups of primitive stone dwellings, as well as hermits' cells, round towers, holy wells and ruined churches.

Inis Oírr (http://discover inisoirr.com) is the smallest island with a beautiful, sandy beach, An innovative arts centre, Aras Eanna (www.araseanna.ie), regularly hosts some of Ireland's top acts, including Tommy Tiernan and Damien Dempsey. Inis Oirr is instantly recognisable to fans of the TV classic 'Father Ted' as Craggy Island, look out for the Tedfest celebrations (www.tedfest.org) every February.

COUNTY MAYO

Rising high above Clew Bay, conical **Croagh Patrick** is Ireland's holy mountain. Every year thousands of pilgrims ascend the imposing summit, most of them on the last Sunday in July. St Patrick is said to have spent Lent here in 441. There are spectacular views of the wide bay and the hills of counties Mayo, Clare and Galway.

Westport ㉜, at the head of Clew Bay, is an example of 18th-century urban planning. The Mall boulevard follows the Carrowbeg River. Outside the town, the home of the Marquess of Sligo can be visited. **Westport House** (daily, usually 10am–6pm but hours vary greatly so check online, closed Jan–Feb; www.westporthouse.ie) is palatial, with paintings, silver and glassware. There is a Pirate Adventure Park with flume rides and dungeons.

Castlebar, a quiet partly Georgian town, is the county town of Mayo. To the east, in Turlough, **The National Museum of Country Life ㉝** (Tue–Sat 10am–5pm, Sun 2–5pm; free; www. museum.ie) houses the National Folklife Collection, a series

CRUISING THE RIVER SHANNON

The best place to hire a boat is Carrick-on-Shannon, the capital of County Leitrim and home to the superb Costello Chapel. Downstream, the river runs into Lough Corry, the first of many interconnected lakes in the Shannon basin. **Lough Ree**, halfway down, is 26km (16 miles) long and 11km (7 miles) wide, with deserted wooded islands.

The main cross-country roads ford the Shannon at the central market town of **Athlone**, with a medieval castle overlooking the Shannon Bridge. The town holds a number of festivals and cultural events. At a bend in the river is **Clonmacnoise**, an ancient monastic settlement founded in the 6th century by St Ciaran. Nearby you can follow a 9-km (5.5-mile) trip along the Clonmacnoise & West Offaly Railway.

Just 6km (4 miles) south of Clonmacnoise, a 16-arch bridge marks Shannonbridge; at Shannon Harbour the Grand Canal from Dublin meets the river. Portumna is a fishing and boating resort with a new marina.

Lough Derg is the largest of the Shannon lakes – 40km (25 miles) long and up to 5km (3 miles) wide with islets and fair green hills beyond – a perfect end to the trip. This is just as well because dangerous rapids abound below **Killaloe**, a prudent place to abandon ship. Killaloe was once a great ecclesiastical centre, where **St Flannan's Cathedral** has been restored to its 12th-century glory. The richly carved Romanesque doorway is said to be the entrance to the tomb of King Murtagh O'Brien of Munster (d. 1120). The granite shaft nearby, from about the year 1,000, bears a bilingual inscription in Runic and Ogham letters – a foretaste of today's Irish-English road signs.

of hugely entertaining displays illustrating rural life in Ireland from 1850 to about 1950.

Inland, the village of **Knock** (from the Irish *Cnoc Mhuire* – 'Mary's Hill') is a respected place of pilgrimage. In 1879 the townspeople saw an apparition of the Virgin Mary, St Joseph and St John on a south gable of the old parish church. In the centenary year of 1979, pilgrim Pope John Paul II came from Rome to address an open-air mass at Knock with over 400,000 of the faithful. Knock still caters to the pilgrims, with souvenir shops and a museum of folklore and handicrafts. The site of the famous apparition has been enclosed in glass, and statues recreate the position of the figures in the vision.

In **Foxford**, the old woollen mill houses an interpretative centre that tells the story of the famine in the area, while near Ballycastle, on the north Mayo cliffs, the pyramid-shaped heritage centre of **Céide Fields** (Apr–May and Oct daily 10am–5pm, until 6pm June–Sept; www.heritageireland. ie) uncovers the site of one of the area's many prehistoric settlements. The site, dating back to 3000 BC, is estimated to be the single largest Stone Age monument in existence in the world today.

SHAMROCK CURTAIN

Travelling in the west of Ireland you may cross the Shamrock Curtain, an important cultural frontier. Signs are printed in Gaelic letters and the people speak Irish as a first language. This is the Gaeltacht. Its residents strive to maintain Irish as a living language. The Dublin government actively supports Gaeltacht efforts to keep the old language and culture alive. Courses in Irish offered here every summer are a rite of passage for Irish teenagers.

The country's biggest island, **Achill** , is buffeted by wind and tide, with meagre farms between ominous mountains and rocky shores. Despite this (or because of it) the scenery – from enormous cliffs to superb beaches – is truly magnificent. Achill feels adrift, though you can drive there from the mainland across an unimpressive bridge. Driving on the island's deserted roads can revive the joy of motoring.

Prehistoric graves can be found on the harsh slopes of Achill's overpoweringly high mountain, the 672-m (2,204-ft) **Slievemore**. Driving offers the most vertigo-inducing cliff views and perspectives of the ocean churning round the off-islands and shoals. Inland, note the three-chimneyed cottages set between moors and bogs.

Sligo town

THE NORTHWEST

Sligo ㉟ lies between two mountains, Ben Bulben and Knocknarea. The Vikings invaded here in 807. In 1252 Maurice Fitzgerald, the Earl of Kildare, founded **Sligo Abbey** (Apr–mid-Oct daily 10am–6pm; www.heritageireland.ie), a Dominican friary. It burned down in 1414, but was soon rebuilt. It was attacked by Puritan troops in 1641, and the friars were killed. Its ruins combine desolation and grace. Three sides remain, and there are fine carvings.

The resort of **Strandhill**, west of Sligo, has a beach with long-rolling waves for surfers. **Knocknarea**, the flat-topped mountain over this stretch of shore, must have had a curious attraction for the early settlers, as the area abounds in megalithic monuments. A steep but manageable climb will bring you to the 328-m (1,078-ft) summit of Knocknarea, where a large cairn is believed to mark the burial place of the 1st-century Queen Maeve of Connaught. This vantage point gives a fantastic, sweeping view across Sligo Bay. Awesome **Ben Bulben** looms in the distance, 526m (1,730ft) high. On its flat top you'll find arctic and alpine plants.

In the shadow of this majestic mountain is the small church of **Drumcliff**, with its turreted belfry. It was the desire of W.B. Yeats, who spent many childhood summer holidays around Sligo, to be laid to rest in the churchyard, 'Under bare Ben Bulben's head'.

Donegal town has a charming setting

About 27km (17 miles) to the north of Sligo, situated on the approach to the village of Mullaghmore, look out for the stunning **Classiebawn Castle**, which claims the skyline all to itself. This was the summer dwelling of Earl Mountbatten of Burma, who was assassinated by the IRA in 1979 when his fishing boat was blown up just off the shore nearby.

Donegal's medieval castle

COUNTY DONEGAL

The most northerly county on the island, **Donegal** is known for its scenery – mountains, glens and lakes. This is also where Donegal homespun **tweed** comes from. **Donegal town** ❸ has a medieval **castle** that occupies the site of a previous Viking fort. (*Dun na nGall* in Irish means the 'Fortress of the Foreigners', a reference to the Vikings.) On the edge of town, the ruins of Donegal Abbey overlook the estuary. West along the coast, **Killybegs** is a big fishing port; the trawlers here have wheelhouses with devices for tracking down the fish.

The road to the village of **Glencolumbkille** ❸ heads deep into spectacular country. Over the crest of a hill, you see the simple village below, enfolded in green hillsides that funnel down to the sea. In Irish the name *Glencolumbkille* means the 'Glen of St Colmcille' (or St Columba).

Today it is said that the 6th-century saint, who changed the course of history by introducing the Christian faith to Scotland, began his career by converting locals. The numerous old **standing stones** were formerly pagan monuments

The Hands Across the Divide statue in Derry

which St Columba simply adapted to the new religion. On the saint's feast day, 9 June, pilgrims follow the pathway of these old stones. Over 40 prehistoric *dolmens, souterrains* and cairns have been catalogued in this area, some as old as 5,000 years.

Perched on a hilltop in Inishowen, you can visit the **Grianan Aileach Ring Fort** dating from 1700BC, it is well-preserved and similar in style to Staigue Fort in County Kerry. **Fort Dunree**, on the Inishowen peninsula overlooking Lough Swilly, is a fascinating military history museum in an old fort.

Glenveagh National Park ③⑧ (Mar–Oct 9am–6pm, Nov–Feb 9am–5pm; www.glenveaghnationalpark.ie) forms 10,000 hectares (24,700 acres) of the most beautiful part of Co. Donegal, with magnificent lakeside views from Glenveagh Castle. Nearby is Glebe House and Gallery (Jun–Oct Sat–Thu 11am–6.30pm; http://glebegallery.ie), an elegant Regency country house and gardens built in 1828 that's worth a look. This was once the home of the artist Derek Hill, who generously bequeathed it along with his impressive art collection to the Irish state in 1981.

NORTHERN IRELAND

Surprisingly for such a historically troubled area, it's sometimes hard to be sure of the exact location of the border between the Republic and Northern Ireland. Partly this is because it snakes its way along 18th-century county boundaries through farming land that is sometimes bleak, more often breathtakingly beautiful, taking little account of natural boundaries such as rivers, or of the cultural differences that separate Republican-minded Roman Catholics and British-oriented Protestants. Houses straddle it so that, as the joke has it, a man may sleep with his head in the United Kingdom and his heart in the Republic of Ireland.

Political expediency accounts for the absurdities. It had been intended to redraw the border rationally after partition in 1920 left six of the nine counties of the ancient province of Ulster (Antrim, Down, Armagh, Derry, Fermanagh and Tyrone) under British rule, and a Boundary Commission was set up. But in the end the British and Irish governments, both hoping to avoid further trouble, suppressed the commission's report and left things as they were. Had they decided differently, much of the subsequent conflict might have been averted.

Shopping in Belfast's bustling centre

BELFAST

Belfast , the capital, looks little different from a provincial English city. Donegall

Place, the 'main street', is lined with UK chain stores; while postboxes are no longer green, as in the Republic, but red. Sectarian tensions are, increasingly, a thing of the past: nowadays bus and taxi tours show visitors where the worst riots of the 1970s and '80s took place.

Set in a saucer of green hills and spanning the mouth of the River Lagan as it flows into the Irish Sea, Belfast is essentially a Victorian creation, its wealth founded on textile manufacturing and shipbuilding. Today most of the factories have vanished, though two towering yellow cranes (Samson and Goliath) survive as a reminder of the great days of Harland & Wolff shipyard, builder of the *Titanic*. The 100th anniversary of the sailing of the pride of Belfast's shipyards, the Titanic took place in April 2011, and was marked by the opening of Titanic Belfast, the world's largest Titanic visitor experience.

Dominating the centre in Donegall Square is the 1906 **City Hall** Ⓐ whose architecture has been dubbed 'Wrenaissance' in tribute to its shameless resemblance to St Paul's Cathedral in London. Queen Victoria presides outside, her statue supported by workers from the linen and shipbuilding industries. Inside, an ornate marble staircase sweeps up to the Rotunda, and the banqueting hall and council chamber are suitably extravagant. Among the marble statues around the City Hall is a **Titanic Memorial**, complete with weeping sea-nymphs.

Queen's University

To the north of the City Hall, Donegall Place, which becomes Royal Avenue, is Belfast's main shopping area. **Linen Hall Library** Ⓑ,

Taking it easy

on Donegall Square North, is a revered public-subscription library – a treasure house for historians and political journalists. Close by, on Great Victoria Street, are two architectural gems: the 1895 **Grand Opera House ⓒ** (www.goh.co.uk), with its plush brass and velvet, its gilded elephant heads and its excellent acoustics, and the **Crown Liquor Saloon ⓓ**, a riot of Victorian Baroque owned by the National Trust but still serving the finest Guinness and whiskies.

Great Victoria Street leads on, via Shaftesbury Square, to the Tudor-style **Queen's University ⓔ**, whose central tower bears a suspicious resemblance to that of Magdalen College, Oxford. The university has colonised just about every available building in the vicinity, but welcome green space is provided by the adjacent **Royal Botanic Gardens ⓕ**, which contain a curvilinear Palm House. Beside the park is the revamped **Ulster Museum ⓖ** (Tue–Sun 10am–5pm; http://nmni.com/um) which is noted for its well-presented displays of art, human history and natural sciences.

The Giant's Causeway

Belfast, of course, has many churches. Worth checking out are the neo-Romanesque **St Anne's Cathedral** in Donegall Street, the extravagantly decorated interior of **St Malachy's Church** in Clarence Street and the delightful **First Presbyterian Church** in Rosemary Street.

Across the River Lagan, in the newly-named Titanic Quarter, the **Odyssey Arena** (www.odysseyarena.com) is a venue for sporting events and pop concerts, and hosts the children's science and discovery centre, W5 (Mon–Fri 10am–5pm, Sat 10am–6pm, Sun noon–6pm; www.w5online.co.uk). One of the city's newer attractions, the **Titanic Belfast** (daily Jan–Mar and Oct–Dec 10am–5pm; Apr–May and Sept 9am–6pm; June–Aug 9am–7pm; www.titanicbelfast.com) relives the liner's story in nine galleries with full-scale reconstructions.

On the Newtownards Road, 10km (6 miles) from the centre, are the much televised **Parliament Buildings** at Stormont. They are now the home of the Northern Ireland Assembly.

THE ANTRIM COAST ROAD

To the northeast of Belfast, past **Carrickfergus** (which has a fine Norman castle) and the industrial port of **Larne ⓐ**, the lovely **Antrim Coast Road** runs alongside the Irish Sea through picturesque villages such as **Cushendall** and **Cushendun**.

The north coast begins at **Ballycastle ⓐ**, setting for the Ould Lammas Fair agricultural fair in August, held since 1606, and the ferry departure point for a 13-km (8-mile) trip to **Rathlin Island**, whose population of 100 is vastly outnumbered by seabirds. Continuing east, you pass **Carrick-a-Rede Rope Bridge** (daily weather permitting Mar–May and Sept–Oct 9.30am–6pm; June–Aug 9.30am–7.30pm; Nov–Feb 9.30am–3.30pm) which swings over a 24-m (80-ft) chasm, allowing salmon fishermen and brave tourists access to a rocky promontory. Past cliffs and white surfers' beaches are

MUSIC AND MURALS

Northern Ireland's popular culture portrays the sectarian divide with the bluntness of bombs and bullets. Triumphalist or threatening murals adorn the sides of hundreds of houses, particularly in Belfast and Derry. The Protestant versions often feature William of Orange, who defeated his Catholic father-in-law, James II, at the Battle of the Boyne in 1690. Catholic murals celebrate Republican heroes and aspirations. Balaclava-clad men brandishing rifles are common to both traditions. The worst murals are crudely executed; the best can be evaluated as folk art.

For both Protestants and Catholics, marching bands keep history alive and mark out territory. The biggest parades are staged on 12 July by Protestant Orangemen (commemorating William of Orange). On the surface it's tuneful pageantry – but it can also be fiercely provocative.

Derry/Londonderry

the romantic ruins of 6th-century **Dunseverick Castle**.

Bushmills is home to the world's oldest distillery (tours and whiskey tastings available). It is also the jumping-off point for Ireland's most spectacular natural phenomenon, the **Giant's Causeway** ㊷. Formed 60 million years ago when molten lava froze into 38,000 basalt columns, mostly hexagonal, it looks like a series of giant stepping-stones. Park near the Causeway or, in season, catch a narrow-gauge steam locomotive from Bushmills. To the west are the resorts of **Portrush** and **Portstewart**, and the ruins of the 14th-century **Dunluce Castle**.

DERRY CITY AND FERMANAGH

Protestants still call **Derry** ㊸, Northern Ireland's second city, Londonderry, the name given to it by the London guilds who began creating the walled city in 1614. The 6-m (20-ft) thick walls boast watchtowers and cannons, such as the 1642 'Roaring Meg'. The excellent **Tower Museum**, in Union Hall Place, relates the city's troubled history. **St Columb's Cathedral**, in London Street, is a graceful 17th-century Anglican church.

3.5km (5 miles) north of Omagh is the **Ulster-American Folk Park** ㊹ (Oct–Feb Tue–Fri 10am–4pm, Sat and Sun

11am–4pm; Mar–June Tue–Sun 10am–5pm; July–Aug daily 10am–5pm; Sept Tue–Sun 10am–5pm; http://nmni.com/uafp). The rebuilt craftsmen's cottages, schoolhouse and forge recreate 18th-century living conditions here, while log cabins and covered wagons illustrate the New World that many emigrants created in America. It is said that 11 US presidents had their roots in the province.

Further south, **Fermanagh** is the province's lakeland playground. Summer pleasure boats ply the lakes from the busy town of **Enniskillen** ⓭. On Lower Lough Erne, **Boa Island** has an ancient two-faced Janus statue, radiating Celtic inscrutability, and **Devenish Island** has a fine round tower.

Heading back towards the east coast, **Armagh** ⓮ has two fine cathedrals (both called St Patrick's), some notable Georgian buildings and a planetarium. Just outside the town is **Navan Fort**, one of Ireland's most important historical sites – the ancient seat of the kings of Ulster.

MOUNTAINS OF MOURNE

Close to the Irish Sea, the 15 granite peaks of the **Mourne Mountains** ⓯ reach to more than 600m (2,000ft). At the summit of Slieve Donard are two cairns (ancient mounds of stones). From here, on a clear day, you can see Scotland, England, the Isle of Man and Snowdonia in Wales.

Passing through **Downpatrick**, you can take the ferry from Strangford to Portaferry and drive up the **Ards Peninsula** ⓰ a 37-km (23-mile) finger dotted by villages and beaches. **Mount Stewart**, an 18th-century mansion, has one of Europe's greatest gardens (Mar–Oct). At Cultra, near Holywood on the main road into Belfast, the **Ulster Folk and Transport Museum** ⓱ (Mar–Sept Tue–Sun 10am–5pm; Oct–Feb Tue–Fri 10am–4pm, Sat and Sun 11am–4pm; http://nmni.com/uftm) is set in 70 hectares (170 acres) of a green and picnic-friendly park.

WHAT TO DO

SPORTS

Whether on land or sea (or river or lake), the Irish enjoy so many sporting activities that we can only touch on a handful of the most popular. If you are interested in more esoteric sports, such as kite-surfing, hang-gliding, or even polo, the tourist board (see page 130) can put you in touch with the appropriate sports associations.

SPORTS ASHORE

Golf. In a country so green, you might scarcely notice the vast number of golf courses, but there are more than 400, including several of championship status. Some clubs are private, but not rigorously so: while you might find that non-members are excluded over the weekend, you'll have few problems on weekdays. See www.golf.discoverireland.ie for more details.

Greyhound racing. This is a very popular pursuit. Teams of hare-brained dogs keep eager gamblers busy six nights a week in Dublin – which has two greyhound stadiums – and elsewhere in Ireland. See www.igb.ie.

Horse racing. Almost everyone in Ireland seems to be totally engrossed, one way or another, in the sport of kings. Dublin boasts several famous courses within easy reach. The flat season is from March to November, and steeplechasing goes on all year. See www.goracing.ie for information on events.

Horse riding. Stables can be found all over Ireland with fine Irish horses, beautiful ponies, and trekking routes through delightful verdant countryside; www.ehi.ie lists establishments that specially cater for holiday makers.

National games. Hurling is a very fast variant of hockey, in which a small, leather ball known as a sliotar is struck with a

Walking in the Mourne Mountains

Riding ponies on Cleggan Beach in Connemara

wooden hurley. Gaelic football, the other traditional Irish game, includes elements of both soccer and rugby. For more information on Gaelic sporting events and history, go to www.gaa.ie.

Imported games. Rugby (www.irishrugby.ie) and football (www.fai.ie) are very popular, while hockey (www.hockey.ie), basketball (www.basketballireland.ie) and cricket (www.cricketireland.ie) also have a following.

Walking and cycling. Both have grown in popularity, with some 32 long-distance walking routes, and dedicated cycle routes, such as the Great Western Greenway (www.greenway.ie) in Co Mayo. See www.discoverireland.ie/walking or www.discoverireland.ie/cycling

SPORTS ON THE WATER

Sailing. Watersports of all kinds are popular in Ireland, with its long indented coastline. Hire a yacht with or without skipper, or get afloat in a simple kayak. See www.discoverireland.ie and www.sailing.ie

Scuba diving. It's popular all around Ireland – mostly in the summer months, as the water can get mighty cold. Along the north coast, there are lots of wreck dives: many believe that Spanish galleons from the Armada are still lurking beneath the waves. For a list of dive centres see www.scuba.ie

Sea fishing. From a long sandy beach, a pier, a clifftop or a boat, you can hook big beautiful trophies of the deep, such as shark, sea bass, tope, skate, halibut, conger and many more. Details at www.discoverireland.ie/angling

Swimming. Blue Flag beaches have to meet certain safety criteria, including having adequate life-saving equipment and, if necessary, lifeguards. For a list of Blue Flag beaches all over Ireland, visit www.blueflagireland.org

Surfing. The heavy Atlantic swells are more impressive on the west coast, where the biggest surfing bases are Lahinch Co. Clare, Strandhill Co. Sligo, Bundoran Co. Donegal, and Tramore Co. Waterford, on the east coast. See www.surf aroundireland.com

Boating. Cruising the inland waterways in a rented cabin cruiser makes a great break, especially on the River Shannon. You can also try more energetic sports such as canoeing or paddleboarding. See www.discoverireland. ie, www.leitrimsurf.ie and www.waterwaysireland.org

Hurling is a popular Gaelic game

Game fishing. Fertile salmon fisheries are mostly restricted, but arrangements can be made – though preferably well in advance. Trout are abundant in rivers and lakes; as with salmon, you will need a licence. Details at www. discoverireland.ie/angling

Celtic details on souvenirs

SHOPPING

Friendly sales staff help make shopping in Ireland a real pleasure. The most appealing products are made by Irish craftsmen in traditional or new styles; the Kilkenny Design Centre in Kilkenny City has a particularly fine range of traditional goods on offer. The Design and Crafts Council's website at www.ccoi.ie is also a good starting point that enables you to research what's available in the area you're visiting.

For clothes or slightly more eclectic souvenirs, Dublin is the place to visit. It offers shoppers everything from upscale boutiques to huge shopping malls. check out the vast **Dundrum Town Centre** (www.dundrum.ie), just outside Dublin city centre, or the more intimate **Powerscourt Centre** (www.powerscourt centre.ie). Grafton Street is the main shopping street, with high street names and fashionable department stores such as the much-loved Brown Thomas (www.brownthomas.com). Other interesting shops include the **House of Names** (www. houseofnames.ie), Nassau Street, whose handmade coats of arms allegedly feature the crests of more than 96 percent of the world's surnames; and **George's Street Arcade** (www. georgesstreetarcade.ie), just off South Great George's, a vibrant indoor market with an eclectic worldwide mix from Greek olives to Peruvian handwoven rugs.

WHAT TO BUY

Aran jumpers. Demand so far exceeds supply that they are now made in mainland factories as well as on the Aran islands. For genuinely handknitted jumpers, go to Blarney Woollen Mills (www.blarney.com) in Cork, Ó'Máille (www.omaille.com) in Galway and Cleo Ltd (www.cleo-ltd.com) in Dublin.

Connemara marble. A rich green, this stone is unique to Ireland. All sorts of souvenirs are made from Connemara marble, especially jewellery.

Chocolate. Buy delicious hand-made chocolates at Butler's Irish Chocolates in Grafton Street, Dublin, and at the Skelligs Chocolate Factory in Ballinskelligs, County Kerry. Try before you buy at the Lir Cafés in Killarney, County Kerry and Carrigaline, County Cork.

Metal working. Enamel bowls, plaques and pendants by master craftspeople.

Crosses. Reproductions of old Christian crosses and St Brigid crosses made out of straw.

Toys. In Dublin, Avoca (www.avoca.com) and Arnotts (www.arnotts.ie) both have extensive toy departments. Current favourites are Hurlóg (http://hurlog.com/), Little Green Dot (www.littlegreendot.ie) and Wild Wood Toys (www.wildwoodtoys.com).

Glassware. Waterford crystal, world renowned, is still available even though the factory has closed. Jerpoint Glass in County Kilkenny produces hand-blown uncut crystal in contemporary designs.

Jewellery. Celtic designs inspire today's goldsmiths and silversmiths, while others work in a contemporary style. In Dublin, head to DesignYard (www.designyard.ie) for high end Irish jewellery.

Lace. Although a waning trade in Limerick and County Monaghan, there is now a strong revival of lacemaking in Carrickmacross, Clones, Kenmare and Youghal.

Linen. Weaving continues in Northern Ireland, with a huge emphasis on quality. Irish Linen should bear the Irish Linen Guild's trademark, see www.irishlinen.co.uk. Brands such as Thomas Ferguson and Baird McNutt are heirloom quality.

Paintings. Artists produce fine studies of Ireland, including landscapes, seascapes, flora and fauna, in oils, watercolours, prints and etchings. Check out Merrion Square (www.merrion art.com) in Dublin every weekend all year round to source unique pieces of art.

Peat. Even the turf of Ireland is compressed and sculpted to reproduce ancient religious and folklore symbols.

Pottery. Traditional and modern designs, sought after by collectors. Kiltrea Bridge Pottery from County Wexford and Nicholas Mosse Pottery from County Kilkenny are always in fashion.

Rushwork. In a land rich in thatched cottages, the makers of woven baskets and similar wickerwork still thrive.

A traditional Irish music performance in the Tigh Neachtain pub, Galway

Smoked salmon. A souvenir you can eat that is specially packed for travelling, and on sale at the airport. Opt for wild salmon that is certified organic.

Souvenirs. Leprechauns, marble worry stones and *shillelaghs* (short wooden clubs) are all widely available. Books about Irish history make easy-to-carry souvenirs. GAA jerseys are a quirky gift – wear your county colours with pride!

Tweed. Handwoven fabrics in a variety of colours and weights, traditionally weaved in Donegal. Check out Magee (www.magee1866.com) on Wicklow St, Dublin and Donegal Woollen Mills (www.donegalwoollenmill.com) in Downings, County Donegal.

Wood turning. Many wood turners use only storm-damaged timber, making an ecologically sound product.

ENTERTAINMENT

TRADITIONAL MUSIC

Many hotels and pubs provide entertainment, featuring the most diverse cross-section of traditional Irish entertainment possible: folk singers, harpists, dancers and storytellers. In local pubs the programme may consist of a lone folk singer with guitar. At the other end of the scale the luxury hotels put on elaborate productions. The shows have a typically Irish mixture of hand-clapping high spirits and 'Come Back to Erin' nostalgia. Jigs and reels are tirelessly danced, and lively tap dancers revive some of the country's oldest and best routines. Harps and banjos, bagpipes and accordions are all played with gusto, and fast fiddlers are as ubiquitous here as gypsy violinists in Budapest.

You will find more genuine versions of traditional Irish music at *fleadhanna*, festivals of music and song around the island, climaxing in the All Ireland *Fleadh* in August. Tourist offices will have detailed schedules of such events (www.fleadhnua.com).

Co Clare's beaches are great fun for children

CLUBS AND BARS

The traditional pub is the heartbeat of Irish life and you can still find the real thing all over the country. Escape the gastro-pubs to traditional drinking holes like Dublin's ancient Brazen Head on Bridge Street Lower and, in Belfast, the Crown Liquor Saloon on Great Victoria Street (see page 83). Both will be full of tourists, but a great experience all the same.

Dublin has a lively clubbing scene, centring on the Temple Bar and Harcourt St areas. The better clubs have world-class DJs nightly, plus regular live acts. The Button Factory (www.buttonfactory.ie) features a wide range of live music, and late-night themed events attracting a young crowd. Older sophisti-cates will enjoy the atmosphere at The Sugar Club on Leeson Street (www.thesugarclub.com).

MEDIEVAL MAYHEM

Restored medieval castles are used for grandiose candlelit **banquets** with traditional stories, poems and songs. These

recreations of lusty celebrations from the past are profes-
sionally arranged. If you don't wish to drive, there are package
tours that include door-to-door transportation. Popular venues
include Bunratty and Knappogue Castles in County Clare and
Dunguaire Castle in County Galway. www.shannonheritage.com

THEATRE

Ireland's grand **theatrical** tradition – which gave the world
Goldsmith, Shaw, Sheridan, Beckett, O'Casey and more
recently Conor McPherson and Martin McDonagh – continues
in major towns such as Dublin, Belfast and Cork. Tickets are
usually available on the night at Ireland's National Theatre,
the Abbey Theatre (www.abbeytheatre.ie) and the Gate
Theatre (www.gatetheatre.ie) in Dublin. See www.entertain-
ment.ie for full listings of concerts, theatre and film.

CHILDREN

Fun activities for children of all ages can be found throughout
the country at:

Bray promenade, 19km (12 miles) south of Dublin. Seaside
resort with dodgems, amusement arcades and a seafront
aquarium.

Bunratty Castle and Folk Park, County Clare, tel: (061) 360
788, www.shannonheritage.com. Costumed guides recreate
life in olden times. Open daily year-round.

Clara-Lara, Vale of Clara, County Wicklow, tel: (0404) 46161,
www.claralara.com. Fun park, trout farm and amusements
for children of all ages. Open summer only.

Imaginosity, Sandyford, County Dublin, tel: (01) 217 6130,
www.imaginosity.ie. A fun and educational space for children.

Dublin Zoo, tel: (01) 474 8900, www.dublinzoo.ie. A wide
variety of animals and educational programmes. Watch the
meerkats play from the Restaurant.

There is plenty to entertain children in Dublin

Exploris, Portaferry, County Down, tel: (028) 4272 8062, www.exploris.org.uk. Discover creatures of the deep.

Farm visits. Many farms open to visitors and are ideal for kids. Tourist offices (see page 130) have details.

National Aquatic Centre, Dublin, tel: (01) 646 4300, www.aquazone.ie. Ireland's biggest swimming pool and best water rides make for a lot of family fun.

Fota Wildlife Park, Carrig-twohill, County Cork, tel: (021) 481 2678, www.fotawildlife.ie. This large park opens year-round.

National Gallery of Ireland, Dublin, tel: (01) 661 5133, www.nationalgallery.ie. Frequent children's activities.

National Wax Museum, Dublin, tel: (01) 671 8373, www.waxmuseumplus.ie. Historical and celebrity wax figures, chamber of horrors.

Newbridge Demesne, County Dublin, tel: (01) 843 6534, www.newbridgehouseandfarm.com. An 18th-century house with farm and animals.

The Steam Museum, Straffan, County Kildare, tel: (01) 628 8412, www.steam-museum.ie, has model and full-sized steam engines; open May–Sept.

Kerry County Museum, tel: (066) 712 7777, www.kerrymuseum.ie, in Tralee has a child-friendly Medieval Experience.

Viking Splash Tours, Dublin, tel: (01) 707 6000, www.vikingsplash.ie. Put on a Viking helmet and explore land and sea in a vintage World War II amphibious vehicle.

CALENDAR OF EVENTS

January: *TradFest Temple Bar*, Dublin – traditional and folk music festival; *Shannonside Winter Music Weekend*, Co Clare – acoustic music.

February: *Dublin International Film Festival*; *Dine in Dublin* – food festival with special offers for restaurants.

March: *St Patrick's Week* – celebrations throughout Ireland; *Dingle International Film Festival*, Co Kerry – special focus on animation.

April: *Pan-Celtic International Festival* – music, song, dance, and cultural events celebrating the Celtic tradition; *Irish Grand National Weekend at Fairyhouse*, Co Meath; *The Cork International Choral Festival*; *West Waterford Festival of Food* – tastings and demonstrations.

May: *Irish Open Golf Championships*; *Fleadh Nua* – traditional music and dance in Ennis, Co. Clare; *Listowel Writers Week*, Co. Kerry; *Slieve Bloom Walking Festival*, Kinnitty, Co Offaly –guided walks in the mountain for all; *Cat Laughs Comedy Festival*, Kilkenny.

June: *Great Music in Irish Houses Chamber Music Festival*, all over Ireland; *Cork Midsummer Festival* – huge arts festival with promenade theatre; *Irish Derby* at the Curragh racecourse, Co. Kildare.

July: *Galway Races*; *Galway Arts Festival*; *Lady of the Lake Festival*, Enniskillen, Co Fermanagh; *Earagail Arts Festival* – music and arts festival throughout Co Donegal in Irish and English.

August: *Connemara Pony Show*, Clifden, Co. Galway; *Kilkenny Arts Festival*; *Oul' Lammas Fair*, Ballycastle, Co. Antrim; *Puck Fair* – parades and family fun in Killorglin, Co. Kerry; *Stradbally National Steam Rally*, Co. Laois; *Rose of Tralee International Festival*, Kerry

September: *GAA All-Ireland Senior Hurling Final*, Dublin; *Clarenbridge Oyster Festival*, Galway; *Lisdoonvarna Matchmaking Festival*, Co. Clare – traditional matchmaking amid much merriment.

October: *Kinsale Gourmet Festival*, Co. Cork; *Dublin Theatre Festival*; *Bram Stocker Festival*, Dublin; *Ballinasloe Fair*, Co. Galway – Europe's oldest horse fair; *Cork Jazz Festival*; *Belfast Festival at Queen's* (arts).

November: *National Circus Festival Ireland*, Tralee, Co Kerry – watch and learn circus skills; *Dublin Beatles Festival* – celebration of the fab four.

EATING OUT

Pubs are popular lunch or dinner spots and they range from traditional taverns serving up sandwiches and salads to cosmopolitan gastro pubs. Cafés provide relaxed brunches and afternoon teas and there are luxurious restaurants offering Michelin-starred cuisine. Vegetarians are pretty well catered for these days, and the trend for locally-sourced artisan food has greatly enhanced the choice at all price levels.

Dublin's days of overcooked cabbage and cholesterol-laden fried meat are long gone. The city is increasingly sophisticated in its array and quantity of restaurants, and is matching other European capitals as a breeding ground for talented and innovative chefs. It can be expensive, though.

Kinsale, a small town in County Cork, and Kenmare, a village in County Kerry have both been called the 'gourmet capital' of Ireland. Cork and Galway have a good choice of casual

Cork's English Market

city centre restaurants, while Belfast takes its culinary reputation seriously, and has a wide choice of adventurous eateries. Outside Dublin and Belfast ethnic restaurants in Ireland tend to be expensive and run-of-the-mill.

Ireland's Blue Book of Country Houses is a good source for exploring Ireland's famous castle hotels and stately homes. Don't miss the chance to enjoy a meal at one of Dublin's top restaurants. Lunch is often half the price of dinner and may include specials.

Alfresco dining

You don't have to look far to find an idyllic setting for a picnic in Ireland. Farmhouse cheeses, smoked salmon, freshly baked bread and fresh produce supply the ingredients. As for the setting, chose from the dramatic winding coastline, romantic forest parks or moody mountain views. The only thing that cannot be guaranteed is the weather.

If you're on a budget, many small cafés and tearooms are good value. Look out for pubs offering 'carvery lunches' – a self-service option with generous portions of the roast of the day, a choice of potatoes, and assorted vegetables for under €10.

There is also the ever-present chippy. Often the traditional end to a night in the pub, they also make a cheap, tasty and quick option to eating out. Thanks to the long coastline, the fish is always fresh and often cooked to order.

In addition to VAT (value added tax, 9 percent in the Republic of Ireland or 20 percent in Northern Ireland), some upmarket restaurants add a service charge to the bill; extra tips are given at about 10 percent of the total bill.

WHEN TO EAT

Breakfast is served from about 7–10am, though in some hotels, matching the general leisurely air, it does not begin until 8am. Lunchtime is from 12.30–2.30pm, give or take half an hour at either end. The time of the evening meal depends on where

Galway Bay oysters

you are. In rural areas and perhaps the less sophisticated town areas, people dine as early as 6pm. In the major towns and cities, however, you can eat any time from 6 or 7–10pm.

WHAT TO EAT

BREAKFAST

A real Irish breakfast starts the day superlatively. You'll feel ready for any kind of exertion after a menu of juice, porridge, or cold cereal with milk or cream, fried eggs with bacon and sausages, toast or tasty homemade soda bread, butter, marmalade, tea or coffee. The quality of the bacon and sausages has improved enormously with the surge in artisan butchers.

In Ulster an important constituent of the breakfast fry-up is fried *farl* (potato bread). Irish soda bread, white or brown, is made from flour and buttermilk, bicarbonate of soda and salt; it's as delicious as cake. Black pudding, a heavy sausage filled with grains and blood, is a treat you'll either love or hate.

OTHER MEALS

Irish **soups** are usually thick and hearty: vegetables, barley and meat stock with a dab of cream, for instance. Look for potato soup made of potatoes, onions, carrots and parsley.

Fish caught fresh from the Atlantic, the Irish Sea or the island's streams is incredibly good. Keep an eye out for some of these great Irish delights: fresh salmon (poached or grilled), smoked salmon, sole and trout from the sea and rivers. Dublin Bay prawns are a big natural resource worthy of their fame, as are Galway oysters (often accompanied by a bottle of stout). With luck you could be offered mussels or lobster, but the great bulk of the catch is usually exported to the Continent.

Meat of the highest quality is at the centre of Irish cuisine. As is common in restaurants around the world, it is generally served simply to allow the fine flavour to speak for itself. The beef is excellent, but there is very little veal. You'll have a choice of roast beef or sumptuous steaks (either T-bone, filet mignon or sirloin) served with elegant sauces, seasonal vegetables and fondant potatoes. Lamb appears as tender chops or as a roast, or the main ingredient in Irish stew, a filling casserole of meat, potatoes, carrots and onions, laced with parsley and thyme. Irish pork products – bacon, sausages, chops and Limerick ham – are also rightly famous. Dublin coddle is a delicious stew of sausages, bacon, onions, potatoes and parsley, a favourite for Saturday night supper in the capital. Venison is another popular choice at quality restaurants, as is rabbit or hare.

Irish stew

Potatoes have been a mainstay of the Irish diet since the 17th century, and a choice of roast, mashed and garlic potatoes or chips with your main course is not unusual. Mushrooms, which thrive in the cool, humid atmosphere here, are the single biggest horticultural export.

More and more restaurants are now serving vegetarian dishes, and fresh produce from Ireland's farms is a dream come true for those thinking Irish food is nothing more than meat and dairy.

Desserts are usually served with lashings of thick cream or ice cream – expect cheesecakes, homemade cakes and tarts, apple pies and crumbles.

WHAT TO DRINK

A jug of tap water is often found on the table, and for many diners it's the only drink during the meal. Ireland has many brands of bottled spring water, widely sold and served in pubs

Galway City's Farmer's Market

and restaurants, and water is gaining popularity as a substitute for alcoholic drinks, especially at lunchtime. Some restaurants have a full licence to serve any drinks; otherwise, they serve wine only and not beer.

The Palace Bar in Fleet Street, Dublin

Irish **pubs** are usually as relaxed and friendly as their regular clients. Most are open all day, and most also serve tea and freshly made coffee. In rural areas the pub may not open until 6pm or later. Closing time is normally around midnight; sometimes later on Friday and Saturday nights. Pubs serving food or providing entertainment can apply for a licence to open later still. Some pubs in Northern Ireland may be shut on Sundays.

The Irish drink nearly 500 million pints of **beer** a year, mostly stout – a rich, creamy, dark brown version. Cork's two brands of stout, Beamish and Murphy's, have become increasingly popular. In many a pub the simple order 'a pint, please' means 568 ml of **Guinness**, lovingly drawn from the keg, scraped and topped. The pouring and settling process takes a little time, but it's worth the wait. The head is so thick that the barman can leave the image of a shamrock sitting within it. A 'glass' of stout means half a pint.

Irish lagers and ales are less filling, and are also worth trying. An interesting Irish drink, **Black Velvet**, combines stout and champagne, and is said to be good for hangovers.

The word **whiskey** comes from the Gaelic *uisce beatha*, 'water of life'. (Purists are at pains to spell Irish whiskey with an 'e' unlike the Scottish version.) Whiskey is matured in wooden casks for at least seven years and is drunk neat,

The Old Jameson Distillery in Smithfield, Dublin

or with a little water – never with ice. You'll see the names of Irish whiskeys etched in the glass of pub windows.

Enthusiasts can visit the world's oldest whiskey distillery, Bushmills (www.bushmills.com), in Northern Ireland; it has held a licence since 1609. There's also the Old Jameson Distillery in Smithfield, the heart of old Dublin, and the Old Midleton Distillery just outside Cork; both are owned by Jameson. For further information go to www.jamesonwhiskey.com.

Whiskey features in many of Ireland's unusual and delicious drinks: **Irish coffee**, in a stemmed glass, is hot coffee laced with whiskey and sugar, with a tablespoonful of thick cream floating on top.

Two Irish liqueurs merit a try: **Irish mist** – honey and herbs in a whiskey base – tingles on the palate, and **Irish cream liqueur**, in different brands, is also very popular with coffee: there's Bailey's and Carolan's, Sheridan's and St Brendan's. It contains whiskey, chocolate and cream – like a leprechaun's milkshake, they say.

PLACES TO EAT

To give you an idea of prices, we have used the following symbols for a three-course meal for one excluding wine:

€€€ over €40   **£££** over £35
€€ €20–40   **££** £15–35
€ under €20   **£** under £15

DUBLIN

Chapter One Restaurant €€–€€€ *18/19 Parnell Square, Dublin 1, tel: (01) 873 2266,* www.chapteronerestaurant.com, *lunch Tue-Fri 12.30–2pm, dinner Tue-Sat 7.30–10.30pm.* This establishment, in the basement of the Dublin Writers Museum, is one of the city's best. The menu is classically French and takes its cheeses and wines very seriously. Located just across from the Gate Theatre, there are pre-theatre menus available from 6pm. Reservations advised.

Cornucopia € *19 Wicklow Street, Dublin 2, tel: (01) 677 7583,* www.cornucopia.ie, *Mon-Tue 8.30am–9pm, Wed-Sat until 10.15pm, Sun noon–9pm.* A small, vegetarian restaurant offering simple, delicious meals such as Turkish bean casserole, tasty salads and wholemeal breads. Great place for breakfast too. Self-service; vegan options available.

Elephant and Castle €–€€ *18 Temple Bar, Dublin 2, tel: (01) 679 3121,* www.elephantandcastle.ie, *Mon-Fri 8am–11.30pm, Sat-Sun 10.30am–11.30pm.* This is the most popular informal restaurant in the city. Quality burgers, salads and brunch options that bring a little bit of New York to Dublin. Vegetarian options.

Ely Winebar €€ *22 Ely Place, St Stephen's Green, Dublin 2, tel (01) 676 8986,* www.elywinebar.ie, *lunch Mon–Thu noon–3pm Fri until 4pm; dinner Mon–Wed 5–10pm,Thu until 10.30pm, Fri–Sat until 11pm.* Experience the elegance of old Dublin in this classic wine-bar restaurant near the Shelbourne Hotel. Over 70 wines served by the glass, and delicious organic food from the family farm.

Fallon & Byrne €–€€ *11-17 Exchequer Street, Dublin 2, tel: (01) 472 1010, www.fallonandbyrne.com, lunch Mon–Sat noon–3pm, Sun noon–4pm; dinner Sun–Tue 6–9pm, Wed–Thu 6–10pm and Fri–Sat 6–11pm.* Organic food emporium in former telephone exchange. Choose from ground floor take-away deli, tapas in the cellar wine bar or classic French brasserie on the spacious top floor.

The Vintage Kitchen €€ *7 Poolbeg Street, Dublin 2, tel: (01) 679 8705, www.thevintagekitchen.ie, lunch Tue–Fri noon–2.30pm, dinner Tue–Sat 5.30–10pm.* Cosy eatery specialising in Irish food and local ingredients. Mouth-watering menus frequently change. Some vintage arts and crafts for sale. It's better to book in advance because the restaurant is rather small. Bring your own wine and there is no corkage charge.

CORK

Ballymaloe House €€€ *Shanagarry, tel: (021) 465 2531, www.ballymaloe.ie, daily lunch 1–2pm and dinner 7–9.30pm (7.30–8.30pm Sun).* This Georgian country house set on 160 hectares (400 acres) also houses a hotel, a cookery school, a craft and specialist kitchenware shop. Run by the Allen family, much noted for their gourmet cooking. Meals are served in the house's cosy dining rooms. Produce is grown in the gardens. The cuisine fits the setting and perfects the tradition of Irish country food.

Jacobs on the Mall €€€ *30a South Mall, Cork, tel: (021) 425 1530, www.jacobsonthemall.com, Mon–Sat 5–10pm.* Local free-range and organic produce are used to create modern European dishes at this airy, contemporary restaurant in Cork City's financial district. There's also a piano bar and private dining room.

Mary Ann's Bar and Restaurant €€ *Castletownshend, County Cork, tel: (028) 36146, www.maryannesbarandrestaurantcork.com, daily 11am–9pm.* Seafood restaurant with cheaper menus served from the bar; the restaurant is set in a small, idyllic seaside village in West Cork. The bar dates back to 1846.

GALWAY

Ard Bia at Nimmo's €–€€ *Spanish Arch, Galway City, tel: (091) 561 114*, www.ardbia.com, *café daily 10am–3.30pm; restaurant daily 6–10pm.* A stone warehouse building on Galway's quayside has a cheerful café with fresh organic food downstairs and a flamboyantly decorated restaurant upstairs serving more formal fare. Great food in a great atmosphere.

The Chop House €€ *Old Malt Arcade, 15 High Street, Galway City, tel: (091) 567 866*, www.thekingshead.ie, *Mon–Sat 12.30–10pm.* A gastro-pub set in a charming courtyard adjoining The King's Head pub. The décor is rustic and the menu focuses on local seafood and steaks, with killer cocktails.

McDonagh's Seafood House €–€€ *22 Quay Street, Galway City, tel: (091) 565 001*, www.mcdonaghs.net, *Mon–Sat 5–10pm (restaurant); Mon–Sat noon–11pm and Sun 2–9pm (fish and chips bar).* Choose between freshly cooked traditional fish and chips or elaborately prepared local seafood, including lobster and scallops, at this long-established Galway institution.

Gaslight Bar and Brasserie €€–€€€ *Hotel Meyrick, Eyre Square, Galway, tel: (091) 564 041*, www.hotelmeyrick.ie, *daily 11am–10pm.* Newly refurbished restaurant overlooking Eyre Square, serving first-class cuisine in bright, airy surroundings. Great place for drinks with an extensive wine list and cocktail menu. A hub for Galway's social scene.

KERRY

Bricin Restaurant €€ *26 High Street, Killarney, tel: (064) 663 4902*, www.bricin.com, *Tue–Sat 6–9pm.* Family-run restaurant serving quality traditional Irish food. Bricin is Gaelic for small trout and is also the name of a well-known bridge in Killarney national park. There is a craft shop for a shot of Irish design.

The Chart House €€ *The Mall, Dingle, tel: (066) 915 2255*, www.the charthousedingle.com, *daily from 6pm, restricted opening off season.* This informal, award-winning cottage restaurant has a warm welcome. The high standard of cuisine concentrates on freshly-landed fish and local artisan food.

Lime Tree Restaurant €€ *Shelbourne Street, Kenmare, tel: (064) 664 1225*, www.limetreerestaurant.com, *Thu–Mon 6.30–9.30pm*. This converted schoolhouse hosts a serious restaurant serving mainstream and modern Irish cuisine. Wide-ranging menu and interesting wine list.

Park Hotel €€€ *Kenmare, tel: (064) 664 1200,* www.parkkenmare. com, *terrace menu daily 6.30–9pm, restaurant daily except for Sun night.* One of Ireland's finest country house hotels, the Park's restaurant uses the finest local produce, prepared in classic French style, served in a relaxing dining area, with views over the lawns to the Caha Mountains.

LIMERICK AND SHANNON

Cullinan's Seafood Restaurant €€ *Doolin, County Clare, tel: (065) 707 4183*, www.cullinansdoolin.com, *Easter–Oct Mon–Tue and Thu–Sat 6–9pm.* A simple, cottage restaurant attached to a small guesthouse, Cullinan's serves fresh local produce, including Burron smoked salmon, Doolin crabmeat, Aran Island scallops, locally-raised lamb and beef, and Irish farmhouse cheeses.

Earl of Thomond Restaurant Dromoland Castle €€€ *Newmarket-on-Fergus, County Clare, tel: (061) 368 144,* www.dromoland.ie, *daily 7–8.30pm.* The dining room in Dromoland Castle is spectacular, with superb, elaborate table settings and grand chandeliers overhead; excellent backdrop for the gourmet cuisine. Smart dress requested.

The Locke Bar and Restaurant €–€€ *George's Quay, Limerick, tel: (061) 413 733,* www.lockebar.com, *Mon–Fri 9am–10pm, Sat–Sun 10am–10pm.* Award-winning gastro-pub that serves breakfast, lunch and dinner 7 days a week. Famous for its seafood, fresh daily specials and traditional Irish music sessions.

The Mustard Seed at Echo Lodge €€€ *Newcastle West Road, Ballingarry, tel: (069) 68508,* www.mustardseed.ie, *daily 6.30–*

9.30pm. Elegant four-course dining in a small Victorian country house hotel.

Sash Restaurant at No. 1 Pery Square €€–€€€ *Pery Square, Limerick, tel: (061) 402 402, www.oneperysquare.com, breakfast daily, lunch Tue–Sun and Dinner Tue–Sat.* On the first floor of this Georgian townhouse is Sash, a reference to the building's Georgian sash windows. This restaurant is stylish yet cosy with a focus on fresh, locally sourced, seasonal ingredients. Wine and artisan food shop.

WATERFORD

Cliff House Hotel €€€ *Ardmore, Co Waterford, tel: (024) 87800 www.thecliffhousehotel.com, restaurant Wed–Sat (Tue–Sat in summer) from 6.30pm, advance booking recommended.* Luxury boutique hotel with sensational cliff top setting and award-winning restaurant for serious foodies and lovers of high style.

Foley's on the Mall €€ *South Mall, Lismore, Co Waterford, tel: (058) 72511, www.foleysonthemall.ie, daily 12.30–8.30pm.* Gastro-pub in a historic building. Heated outdoor area with music in the Summer months. Good value for money with excellent service.

The Strand Inn €–€€ *Dunmore East, Co Waterford, tel: (051) 383 174, www.dunmoreeast.com, breakfast and lunch from 8am until late.* Situated beside a former smuggler's cove, this 300-year-old inn specialises in superb fresh seafood, seasonal produce and homemade desserts. There's also a lively pub with music.

The Tannery Restaurant €€€ *10 Quay Street, Dungarvan, tel: (058) 45420, www.tannery.ie, dinner Tue–Thu 5.30–9pm, Fri–Sat until 9.30pm; lunch Fri 12.30–2.30pm, Sun 12.30–3.30pm.* One of the country's most stylish restaurants in a converted leather warehouse.

WEXFORD

Beaches at Kelly's Resort Hotel €€ *Rosslare, tel: (053) 913 2114, www.kellys.ie, lunch Sun–Sat 1–2pm; dinner Sun–Fri 7.30–9pm, Sat*

7–9pm. Reservations are essential at this firm favourite of both locals and tourists alike. The food is delicious, and the wine list is enticing. Smart dress requested in the evening.

Dunbrody Country House Hotel €€€ *Arthurstown, New Ross, tel: (051) 389600, www.dunbrodyhouse.com, bar menu daily lunch and dinner, restaurant Mon–Sat 6.30–8.30, Sun 1.30–3.30.* A blend of classical Irish cooking and continental charm served in the Harvest Room, which overlooks an organic vegetable and fruit garden. The more informal Seafood Champagne Bar serves favourites such as beer-battered fish and chips.

Marlfield House Hotel €€€ *Courtown Road, Gorey, tel: (053) 942 1124, www.marlfieldhouse.com, Sun lunch 12.30–2.30pm, Wed–Sun afternoon tea 12.30–5pm, dinner 7–9pm but restricted opening off-season.* The menu at this renowned country house is classic French with a twist. Fish, including wild salmon, Bannow Bay oysters and Wexford mussels, is a strong point. Fresh herbs, vegetables and fruit are picked from Marlfield's own gardens. A delightful experience.

WICKLOW

Darcy McGees €€ *Main Street, Arklow, tel: (0402) 91556, www.darcymcgeesatthespawell.ie, daily noon–10pm.* A full carvery available on a daily basis, a wide array of sandwiches plus a la carte menu in the evenings.

The Hungry Monk €€ *Church Road, Greystones, tel: (01) 287 5759, www.thehungrymonk.ie, bistro Mon–Fri 5–11pm, Sun 12.30–9pm, restaurant Fri–Sat 5.30–11pm.* Intimate, candlelit restaurant in a seaside village, specialising in seafood in summer, wild game in winter. Extensive wine list and craft beer menu. Lively fun atmosphere.

Hunter's Hotel €€–€€€ *Newrath Bridge, Rathnew, tel: (0404) 40106, www.hunters.ie, daily lunch 1–2.30pm, afternoon tea 4–5.30pm, dinner 7.30–9pm.* Hunter's Hotel is an historic 18th-century coaching inn with fine gardens. The food here is simple but impressive traditional Irish fare.

The Roundwood Inn ££ *Roundwood, tel: (01) 281 8107, bar food daily 12.30–8.30, restaurant Fri–Sat 7.30–9pm, Sun 1–2pm.* Atmospheric old inn serving local produce from lamb to venison. Good bar food, including goulash, Irish stew and smoked salmon. Reservations necessary for the restaurant.

NORTHERN IRELAND

4 Vicars Restaurant ££ *4 Vicars' Hill, Armagh BT61 7ED, tel: (028) 375 27772, www.4vicars.com, Wed–Sat 10am–4pm, Sun 10am–3pm, Fri–Sat 6.30–9pm.* Conveniently located directly opposite an ancient cathedral, the restaurant offers a small but exceptionally well-tailored local menu.

Howard Street ££ *56 Howard Street, Belfast BT1 6PG, tel: (028) 9024 8362, www.howardstbelfast.com, Tue–Sat noon–2.30pm and 5–9.30pm.* Hip restaurant serving delicious locally sourced dishes.

Madison's £–££ *59–63 Botanic Avenue, Belfast BT7 1JL, tel: (028) 9050 9800, www.madisonshotel.com. Mon–Sat noon–9pm, Sun 1–5pm.* This lively boutique hotel, restaurant and bar features traditional Irish cuisine with a cosmopolitan twist. Conveniently located close to Queen's University.

The Percy French Pub and Bistro ££ *Hastings Slieve Donard Hotel, Downs Road, Newcastle, County Down BT33 0AH, tel: (028) 4372 3175, www.hastingshotels.com, daily noon–9.30pm.* A welcoming and popular venue, serving pub lunch and dinner fare. More formal meals in the Oak Room.

Saltwater Brig ££ *43 Rowreagh Rd, Kircubbin, County Down BT22 1AR, tel: (028) 4273 8435 www.saltwaterbrig.com, daily lunch and dinner.* This family-run pub and restaurant has unbeatable views of Strangford Lough and the Mountains of Mourne. Traditional fare prepared with fresh, local ingredients. Sunday roast is very popular.

Deane's Meat Locker £££ *28–40 Howard Street, Belfast BT1 6PF, tel: (028) 9033 1134, www.michaeldeane.co.uk, Mon–Sat noon–3pm and 5.30–10pm.* Deane's Restaurant offers one of the most memorable fine-dining experience in Belfast in striking minimalist surroundings.

A–Z TRAVEL TIPS

A Summary of Practical Information

A

ACCOMMODATION (See also Camping, Youth Hostels, and the selection of Recommended Hotels starting on page 134)

While exploring Ireland you can stay in different types of accommodation: a luxury hotel one night, a family-run guesthouse the next, or a farmhouse and thatched cottage. Efficient tourist offices will handle both spur-of-the-moment or long-range reservations for you in tourist board approved accommodation. Alternately, visit www.ireland.com or www.discoverireland.ie for accommodation offers and good-value inclusive packages. Tariffs are government-controlled, and the maximum rate which proprietors may charge is displayed in all hotel rooms.

Hotel bills sometimes include a service charge, and you will find that VAT (value added tax) on the total cost of accommodation, meal and service is included in the rates.

Hotels and motels. These are graded by the tourist authorities into five-star ratings.

***** Most luxurious, highest standard of cuisine and services.

**** Extremely comfortable, with many amenities and fine dining.

*** Well-furnished, with private bath and many amenities.

** Well-kept, limited but good cuisine and service, most with private bath.

* Clean, comfortable, hot and cold running water, some ensuite.

The Irish Hotels Federation (www.irelandhotels.com) and the Northern Ireland Hotels Federation (www.nihf.co.uk) list associated hotels. B&B Ireland (www.bandbireland.com) is the major association of bed and breakfast providers. The Irish Self-Catering Federation (www.iscf.ie) and the Northern Ireland equivalent (www.nischa.co.uk) list registered providers, including thatched cottages.

AIRPORTS

International flights arrive at Dublin, Cork, Shannon, Knock and Belfast. Flights also operate from some UK airports to Kerry, Galway, Waterford, Donegal, City of Derry and Sligo.

Dublin Airport, (DUB, tel: (01) 814 1111; www.dublinairport.com) 11km (7 miles) north of the Republic's capital, is the busiest. Aircoach provides air-conditioned coaches with free Wi-Fi to the city centre, South Dublin, Bray, Greystones, Cork and Belfast. Prices start from €6 if you prebook online, see www.aircoach.ie. However you go, the trip takes between half an hour and an hour. Taxi time between the airport and central Dublin is also about half an hour.

Shannon Airport (SNN, tel: (61) 712 000; www.shannonairport.com), one of the first Atlantic gateways, is situated about 24km (15 miles) to the west of Limerick. JJ Kavanagh & Sons provide coaches to Limerick, Nenagh and Dublin Airport. Prices from €5, see http://jjkavanagh.ie/.

Belfast International Airport (Aldergrove, BFS, tel: (028) 9448 4848; www.belfastairport.com) is 24km (15 miles) west of the city. A bus service to town operates every 30 minutes and costs £7.50. Airporter coaches link both of Belfast's airports with Derry, see http://airporter.co.uk. Prices start at £20.

George Best Belfast City Airport (BHD, tel: (028) 9093 9093; www.belfastcityairport.com) is handily situated near the city's old docklands, only 5km (3 miles) from Belfast City Centre. Buses run every 20 minutes and cost £2.50.

B

BICYCLE HIRE

Bikes are easy to rent. See www.discoverireland.ie/cycling for dealer contacts. The hugely popular dublinbikes (www.dublinbikes.ie) is a public bicycle hire scheme, which is free for the first 30 minutes.

BUDGETING FOR YOUR TRIP

Average prices in euros with British pounds where applicable.
Accommodation: (based on bed and breakfast in a standard dou-

ble room in low–high seasons) luxury hotel over €200 (£150)–mid-range hotel €100–200 (£80–150); guesthouse/bed and breakfast €30–100 (£25–80).

Airport transfer: Dublin Airport to city centre by bus €7 (£5), by taxi €30 (£25) plus tip; Belfast International to city centre by bus £6, taxi £25; Belfast City Airport to city centre by bus £2.50, taxi £8.

Bicycle rental: about €75 (£60 per week, plus deposit).

Buses: local fares €4.30 (to the most distant suburb). An eight-day out of 16 Open-Road pass (bus only) covering the Republic of Ireland is €142.50 (www.buseireann.ie), a five-day Tourist Rambler bus ticket for the greater Dublin area costs €29.50. Belfast Metro bus fares start from £2 for short journeys within the city up to £15 for a Smartlink Card giving you up to 10 journeys within the city and its outskirts.

Camping: around €9 (£7) per person per night for a tent pitch.

Entertainment: Cinema tickets cost around €10 (£7.3). Admission prices for nightclubs are €/£5–20 or more. Theatre tickets are €15–60 (£13–50).

Ferry: Galway–Aran Islands €25 roundtrip.

Meals and drinks: Expect to pay €25–65 (£20–54) per person for dinner with wine and coffee; up to €5.50 (£4.80) for a pint of Guinness, €5 (£4) for a pint of beer.

Museums, stately homes: €5–12 (£4.30–10).

Taxis: two-mile taxi journey in Dublin €10. You may find a supplement is payable for extra passengers, baggage, etc.

Tours: Dublin hop-on, hop-off bus tour €15-20. Bus tour around Ring of Kerry from Killarney €25. Belfast City Black Taxi Tour, £25 for up to two people (75 mins).

Trains: Dublin–Cork from €78 return.

C

CAMPING

Officially-approved campsites range from spartan to luxurious. Many a farmer will let campers stay on his property, but always ask first. Hiring camper vans is increasingly popular, see www.bunkcampers.com. If you are bringing your own caravan, note that the connections for Calor gas tanks are not suitable for the cylinders sold in Ireland. Lists of camping and caravanning parks and their facilities are available from tourist information offices or the Irish Caravan and Camping Council (www.camping-ireland.ie). Contact the Northern Ireland Tourist Board; tel: (028) 9023 1221; www.discovernorthernireland.com.

Horse-drawn caravans, most commonly found in west and southwest Ireland, can be rented by the week to sample the gypsy life. Book in advance through www.irishhorsedrawncaravans.com.

CAR HIRE (See also Driving in Ireland)

Car rental companies operate at airports and in towns. International firms usually have slightly higher rates than their local competitors. Some companies permit cars to be picked up in one place and returned elsewhere.

Most companies have a two-tiered tariff, raising prices by up to 20 percent for the summer season. In any season, cars may be rented on either a time-plus-mileage basis or with unlimited mileage, but if you're unsure whether you'll be chalking up enough travelling to justify the unlimited rate, the firm may agree to let you choose the more favourable tariff retroactively. Investigate before you travel.

A valid national licence, normally at least two years old, is required. Many car rental companies permit 21-year-old drivers to hire cars, but the minimum age can be up to 25. The maximum age, depending on the company, ranges from 65 to 70. Credit cards are usually the preferred means of payment.

Rentals begin at around €25 (£18.5) per day or €135 (£100) per week for a small car, including third party insurance, unlimited mileage and taxes. Add about €10 per day for collision damage waiver. Additional coverage can be arranged on the spot, and comprehensive coverage is recommended.

CLIMATE AND CLOTHING

The Gulf Stream is credited with keeping the Irish weather mild year-round, but the unexpected can happen with readings as cold as -19°C (-2°F) and as hot as 33°C (92°F) recorded over the past century. May is usually the sunniest month of the year, and December the dullest. Average monthly temperatures in Dublin:

	J	F	M	A	M	J	J	A	S	O	N	D
°F	41	41	43	47	51	56	59	58	56	50	45	43
°C	5	5	6	8	11	13	15	14	13	10	7	6

Temperatures do not vary much from north to south, but the weather in the west and southwest can be a good deal wetter than elsewhere because the winds come in direct from the sea. Pack some light protective clothing for the summer, and warmer items in the winter.

In the winter the Wicklow Mountains near Dublin, Donegal in the northwest and County Kerry in the southwest have heavy snowfalls, making the territory dangerous even for seasoned walkers and climbers. Wear warm, protective clothing, inform the hotel owners of your route and time of return and take some provisions with you.

CRIME (See also Emergencies and Police)

The Crime Prevention Office of the Garda Siochana (police) warns visitors to carry a minimum of cash and jewellery. Pickpockets do operate in shops and public places. Park in well-lit, busy areas. The Irish Tourist Assistance Service (ITAS) supports tourists who have been the victim of crime, see http://itas.ie/.

D

DISABLED TRAVELLERS

A lot of progress has been made in recent years to provide more facilities for travellers with disabilities. Ramps have been provided, giving access to many community buildings, and much of the public transport system has been adapted. The more modern buses in Dublin have facilities for wheelchair users, and trains have level entry access. The Accessible Ireland website lists attractions which are wheelchair friendly, see www.accessibleireland.com.

DRIVING (See also Car Rental and Emergencies)

Drive on the left and give way to traffic from the right.

Taking your own car. Be sure to have the registration papers and insurance coverage. Virtually any valid driving licence from any country is recognised in Ireland. If yours doesn't include a photograph, keep your passport with you when driving.

Speed limits. Unless otherwise marked, the speed limit in the Irish Republic is 50kmh (30mph) in towns, 80kmh (50mph) on local roads, 100kmh (62mph) on national roads and dual carriageways and 120kmh (74mph) on motorways. In Northern Ireland: 30mph (50kmh) in towns, 60mph (86kmh) on local roads, and 70mph (44kmh) on national roads, dual carriageways and motorways.

Fuel. In some areas finding a petrol station open on a Sunday morning may be a problem, so it's best to top up on Saturday for weekend excursions. Petrol (gas) is sold by the litre.

Seat belts. Drivers and front-seat passengers must wear seat belts in the Republic and Northern Ireland; failure to use them may be punished by a fine. If a vehicle is built with rear seat belts, it is compulsory to use them.

Drinking and driving. Random breath tests are used in certain areas. Those who fail risk heavy fines or jail or both. This affects visitors as well as residents.

Road signs. The road direction signs in the Republic are mostly bilingual, in English and Gaelic. Road signs give distances in kilometres in the Republic and miles in Northern Ireland.

E

ELECTRICITY

The standard current everywhere is 220v, 50AC, but you will find that hotels usually have special sockets for shavers, running at both 220 and 110v. It is possible for certain appliances to need a converter, and also adapter plugs may be required to fit into Ireland's two types of wall outlets. These can be either three-pin flat or two-pin round.

EMBASSIES AND CONSULATES

Australia: Fitzwilton House, Wilton Terrace, Dublin 2; tel: (01) 664 5300; www.ireland.embassy.gov.au

Canada: 7–8 Wilton Terrace, Dublin 2; tel: (01) 234 4000; www.canada.ie

Great Britain: 29 Merrion Road, Dublin 4; tel: (01) 205 3700; www.britishembassyinireland.fco.gov.uk

US: 42 Elgin Road, Dublin 4; tel: (01) 668 8777; http://dublin.us embassy.gov

In Northern Ireland:

US: Danesfort House, 223 Stranmillis Road, Belfast BT9 5GR; tel: (028) 9038 6100; www.usembassy.org.uk/nireland.

EMERGENCIES (See also Embassies and Health)

To contact the police, fire department, or an ambulance in the Republic or Northern Ireland, dial **999 or 112** and tell the emergency operator which service you need. Have details of your location ready before you make your call.

G

GAY AND LESBIAN TRAVELLERS

The general attitude of people in Ireland tends to be tolerant towards gays and lesbians, but travellers may find there is a more conservative attitude in some of the more provincial or remote areas of the country. Same-sex marriage is legal in Ireland.

Various organisations provide advisory services for gay people. They include the **Gay Switchboard** (www.gayswitchboard.ie), and the Dublin **Lesbian Line** (www.dublinlesbianline.ie).

GETTING THERE

From Great Britain

By Air.Visitors and tourists can fly in from airports across the UK to Dublin, Shannon, Cork, Kerry, Galway, Waterford, Donegal, Sligo and Knock in the Republic and to Belfast International, George Best Belfast City and Derry airports in Northern Ireland. New routes are opening all the time, so it may be worth checking with the airline of your choice for information on the most convenient connections.

Charter Flights and Package Tours. Some airlines offer fly-drive tours, as well as special fares which may include your flight and all the transport to and from your final destination in Ireland. Check with the airline of your choice.

Regional Flights. If your time in Ireland is short, you may consider domestic flights between regions. These are operated by Aer Lingus, tel: 1890 800 600 (Ireland) or 0333 004 5000 (UK).

By Sea. Passenger and car ferries sail frequently from Britain to Ireland. There are services from: Holyhead to Dublin, Liverpool and Isle of Man to Dublin and Belfast, Fishguard and Pembroke to Rosslare, Cairnryan and Troon (Scotland) to Larne (near Belfast) and Stranraer to Belfast.

The main ferry operators include Irish Ferries (www.irishferries. com), P&O Irish Sea (www.poirishsea.com), Stena Line (www.stena line.co.uk) and Steam Packet Company (www.steam-packet.com). Schedules and contact numbers are posted on the companies' websites. Pets can travel between the UK and Ireland by car without going through quarantine.

From North America By Air

Travellers from almost every major American city and several major

Canadian cities can make connections to Dublin, Shannon, Belfast or Knock, either direct, or via New York, Chicago or Boston.
Charter Flights and Package Tours. Charter flights to Shannon, with connections to Dublin, feature even further air-fare reductions.

GUIDES AND TOURS

Guided tours are conducted at some major attractions as part of the admission fee, and a variety of excursions are led by guides, covering major monuments and beauty spots by bus. Tourist offices have schedules; the Tourist Office Dublin at 37 College Green, Dublin 2, tel: (01) 410 0700, www.touristofficedublin.com and **Fáilte Ireland** (the National Tourist Development Authority) at 88-95 Amiens Street, Dublin 1, tel: (01) 884 7101, www.failteireland.ie have a list of qualified guides. See also www.discoverireland.ie.

H

HEALTH AND MEDICAL CARE (See also Emergencies)

Residents of EU countries are covered by reciprocal health care in the Republic and in Northern Ireland, and visitors should be sure to bring their European Health Insurance Card (EHIC), which replaced the old E111 form. Other nationalities should have some form of medical insurance – most travel insurance policies provide adequate cover.

Hotels and pharmacies usually know which local doctors are available, but in an emergency dial **999 or 112** to find a doctor on call. VHI Swift Care Clinics (tel: 1890 866 966; www.vhi.ie/swiftcare) provide walk-in urgent care centres in Dublin and Cork. The Dental Hospital, 20 Lincoln Place, Dublin 2, tel: (01) 612 7200, will treat emergency cases.

Pharmacies (chemists) operate during shopping hours. A few stay open until 10pm; in Belfast many are open on Sundays, while in the Republic only some are open for limited hours.

L

LANGUAGE

English is spoken everywhere in Ireland. In the Gaeltacht areas of the west and south, the principal language is Irish, though everyone can speak English too. Bilingualism is officially encouraged. For short language learning courses in the Gaeltacht, visit www.gaelsaoire.ie or tel: 1800 621 600 (Republic of Ireland) or 0800 783 5708 (UK).

Here is a short Irish glossary to help you read the signs:

Irish/Gaelic English

Áth ford of river

baile, bally hamlet, group of houses, town

beann, ben mountain peak

cairn mound of stones atop a prehistoric tomb

carrick, carrig rock

cather fort

clachan, clochan small group of dwellings; stepping stones across a river; beehive-shaped hut

corrach marsh or low plain

derry, dare oak tree or wood

donagh church

drum, drom ridge, hillock

dun, doon fort

ennis, inch, innis(h) island

kil, kill, cill church; monk's cell

lough lake, sea inlet

sceillig, skellig crag, rock

sliabh, slieve mountain

tulach, tully hillock

Here are some handy phrases, with a rough guide to pronunciation:

Dia dhuit hello *diah guich*

slán goodbye *slawn*

oiche mhaith good night *e-ha wah*

go raibh maith agat thank you *goh rev moh a-gut*
le do thoil please *leh doh hol*
tá fáilte romhat you're welcome *taw faltcha rowet*
sláinte! cheers! *sloyn-tcha*
gabh mo leithscéal excuse me *gaw mah leshkale*
Cá bhfuil an ... ? Where is the ... ? *koh will on*
fir/mná men/women *fear/min-aw*

M

MEDIA

Radio and Television. In the Republic, state-run Radio Telefís Éireann (RTE) is the largest broadcaster, though cable and digital television has expanded the choice and includes standard British stations. Most programmes are in English except for a few Irish or bilingual ones. RTE operates three radio stations mainly in English, TG4 in Irish, as well as Raidio na Gaeltachta with an all-Irish programme. In Northern Ireland, the BBC runs five radio stations and two TV stations alongside ITV and Channel Four.

Newspapers. Popular daily broadsheets are the *Irish Independent*, the *Irish Times* and the *Irish Examiner* and, in Northern Ireland, the *News Letter* and the *Belfast Telegraph*.

Entertainment news is covered in the *Herald* of Dublin, the *Evening Echo* of Cork and the *Belfast Telegraph*. Sunday papers, such as the Sunday Independent, are also useful, and visitors will find a what's on section in the Friday edition of the *Irish Times*.

Irish editions of Britain's national daily and Sunday newspapers are sold almost everywhere in both countries on the morning of publication. Leading newsagents in the major towns also sell international newspapers and magazines.

MONEY

Currency. The unit of currency used in the Irish Republic is the euro (€); in Northern Ireland the British pound sterling (£) is used. Both are divided into 100 units. These units are called cents in the Republic, pence in the north. Euro banknotes are issued in €5, €10, €20, €50, €100 and also €500 denominations. Coins come in 1, 2, 5, 10, 20 and 50 cents and 1 and 2 euro.

Exchange facilities. All major banks and many building societies provide exchange facilities. Major post offices, including the GPO in Dublin, have a bureau de change. Some international travel agencies also change money and travellers' cheques. Be sure to bring photo ID when cashing travellers' cheques (see also page 126).

The Suffolk Street Dublin Tourism Office and Visit Belfast Welcome Centre on Donegall Square North operate money exchange services. **Credit cards** are widely accepted.

O

OPENING HOURS

The opening hours of shops and offices can vary from season to season and according to where they are located.

Shops In the cities are normally open from 9am–6pm Mon to Sat and often on Sunday afternoons; country towns have one early closing day. Big shopping centres often stay open until 9pm on Thu and Fri. Smaller shops, particularly grocers and newsagents, often open on Sun and many stay open until 11pm.

Offices and businesses mostly operate from 9am–5.30pm Mon to Fri. Tourist information offices usually open from 9 or 10am–5pm with longer summer hours in the busiest places.

Banks. In general banks open 9.30am–4pm Mon to Fri in the Republic. Most towns have a late opening day once a week (Thu in Dublin), when banks open until 5pm. Most remain open over the lunch hour. Northern Ireland banks have similar opening hours, although outside Belfast, branches may close for lunch.

Pubs. In the Republic, the hours are generally 10.30am–11.30pm during the week, with an extra hour Thu–Sat. On Sun they can open at noon and stop serving at 11pm. In addition, there is half an hour drinking up time in the evenings all year round. All pubs are closed, by law, on Christmas Day and Good Friday. In Northern Ireland, pubs are usually open Mon to Sat 11.30am–11pm, and on Sundays from 12.30–10pm, again with half an hour drinking up time. You may still find some pubs shut on a Sunday.

Museums and stately homes. Museums and stately homes follow no general rule except that visiting hours will often be curtailed in winter. There are no universal days when these institutions are closed, though Sun, Mon, or Tue are the most probable. To avoid disappointment always check first with the nearest tourist information office.

P

PHOTOGRAPHY

Be sure to ask permission before you take photos in museums and historic churches; sometimes flash is forbidden. Military bases (and installations of security forces in Northern Ireland) are off-limits to photographers.

POLICE (See also Emergencies)

The civic guard (police force) of the Irish Republic is the Garda Siochana, known as the Garda (pronounced 'gorda'). The Police Service of Northern Ireland performs similar duties in the North. In case of emergency, telephone 999 or 112, in both the Republic and Northern Ireland.

POST OFFICES

An Post operates all mail services offered in the Republic. Most mailboxes are pillar-shaped and painted green. Most post offices are open from 9am–5.30pm, but the main one – the historic General Post Office in O'Connell Street, Dublin – is open Mon–Sat 8.30am–6pm. Smaller post offices close from 1pm–2pm. Postcard shops and newsstands sometimes sell stamps too. In some areas a post office may be identified by a sign in Irish only – *Oifig an Phoist.*

In Northern Ireland the mailboxes are red. Note that Republic of Ireland stamps cannot be used on mail posted in Northern Ireland and British stamps are invalid in the Republic.

PUBLIC HOLIDAYS

Banks and businesses are closed on public holidays, though some shops and restaurants may stay open. If a date falls on a Sunday, then the following Monday is taken in lieu.

In the Republic of Ireland and Northern Ireland:
1 January New Year's Day
17 March St. Patrick's Day
March/April (movable date) Good Friday/Easter Monday
first Monday in May May Day
25 December Christmas Day
26 December Boxing Day
In the Republic of Ireland only:
first Monday in June June Bank Holiday
first Monday in August August Bank Holiday
last Monday in October October Bank Holiday
In Northern Ireland only:
last Monday in May Spring Bank Holiday
12 July Orangemen's Day
last Monday in August Summer Bank Holiday

R

RELIGION

About 87 percent of the people in the Irish Republic are Catholic. Many but by no means all go to Sunday Mass, which can be heard in Dublin any time from 6am–9pm. Dublin's cathedrals are (Anglican) Church of Ireland, and schedules of the services at these and other Protestant churches can be found in hotels, and in Saturday papers. Dublin has Protestant, Greek Orthodox, Jewish, Islamic, Hindu, Buddhist and Sikh places of worship.

In Northern Ireland, Catholics make up just under half of the population, outnumbering the largest single Protestant group, the Presbyterians, as well as the Church of Ireland and the Methodist church. The ecclesiastic capital of Ireland is Armagh, situated in the North with two cathedrals, one Catholic and the other Church of Ireland. Both are called St Patrick's.

T

TELEPHONES

In the Republic public phone booths are becoming increasingly hard to find as mobiles take over. They are marked in Gaelic, *Telefon*. In Northern Ireland, public telephones are found in metal and glass booths or yellow cubicles. Both generally accept coins and cards.

Most payphones in Ireland take pre-paid phone cards from local post offices and shops. Dial 10 for operator assistance.

Only mobiles with multi-band GSM will work in Ireland. If your phone is non-GSM contact your provider before travelling. It may be cheaper to buy a local SIM card and top up with prepaid calls. If you are coming from the UK your mobile should work in Northern Ireland. You will need international roaming in the Republic.

The international dialling code for the Republic of Ireland is 353, drop the initial zero of the local STD code or mobile number. Northern Ireland is 44 as it is part of the UK. The local code for Northern Ireland is 028, from the Republic you can dial 00 44 28 or simply dial 048 followed by the eight-digit number.

TIME ZONES

Ireland sets its clocks one hour ahead of GMT from mid-March to the end of October, but the rest of the year the clocks are set to GMT.

TIPPING

Some hotels and restaurants include a service charge, so tipping is unnecessary. If not, 10 percent of the bill in a restaurant and a couple of euros a day for cleaners is expected in both the Republic and Northern Ireland. Taxis are usually tipped by simply rounding up the fare.

TOILETS

Gender signs on doors in the Republic may be printed in Gaelic, not English. *Mná* is Gaelic for ladies; *fir* means gentlemen.

TOURIST INFORMATION OFFICES

Tourist information offices and Discover Ireland Centres all over Ireland provide full travel information and advice, booklets, maps and a comprehensive hotel reservation service (for a small charge). The offices are usually open from 9 or 10am–5 or 6pm, although many local ones operate only in the summer. For enquiries, contact:

Fáilte Ireland (the National Tourist Development Authority), 88-95 Amiens Street, Dublin 1, tel: (01) 884 7101, www.failteireland.ie, www.discoverireland.ie

Northern Ireland Tourist Board, St Anne's Court, 59 North Street, Belfast BT1 1NB; tel: (028) 9023 1221; www.discovernorthern ireland.com. You may also address your enquiries to offices of the **British Tourist Authority** the world over, www.visitbritain.com.

TRANSPORT (See also Money)

Buses. The state-run Bus Éireann operates an extensive network of local, provincial and express bus routes in the Republic, including full cross-border services in conjunction with Northern Ireland's Ulsterbus Ltd. Services to tourist destinations increases in summer. Fares and schedule information can be downloaded from www.buse ireann.ie. Expressway buses provide a non-stop inter-city service, while Provincial vehicles make frequent stops in rural areas.

Dublin Bus *(Bus Atha Cliath)* runs services in the Dublin area. For information, tel: (01) 873 4222, www.dublinbus.ie. Dublin Area Rapid Transit (DART) provides a swift and frequent rail link through the city, from Howth in the north to Greystones in the south. For information on fares and schedules, see www.irishrail.ie/dart. The Luas tram system also provides light rail service to outlying suburbs, tel: 1850 300 604, www.luas.ie.

Bus Éireann sell Open Road passes – allowing flexible cross-country travel for varying periods – eg three days out of six, right up to 15 days out of 30. There is also a Rover ticket, which allows up to 15 days of unlimited travel in the Republic, and includes the use of Ulster-bus in Northern Ireland. Or you can buy tickets for combined bus and rail travel: the Explorer pass, for example, is valid in the Republic only.

Trains. Cross-country services to and from Dublin are both quick and comfortable. The main inter-city routes have air-conditioned, sound-proofed expresses. City Gold (First Class) is only available on intercity Dublin-Cork trains and the Dublin-Belfast route has First Plus. Irish Rail *(Iarnród Éireann)* operates trains in the Republic; tel: (1850) 366 222, www.irishrail.ie. In Northern Ireland, Translink operates North-ern Ireland Railways, Enterprise (Belfast–Dublin train service), Ulster-bus (inter-urban), Metro bus (Belfast City) and Goldline (coach); tel: (028) 9066 6630; www.translink.co.uk. Train timetables are available at railway stations and tourist offices, and are also posted on the rail companies' websites.

Note: Dublin has two main-line railway stations (Heuston and Connolly), as well as a commuter-line station, so be sure to check in advance for the correct terminal.

Travellers can use the **Eurail Pass** in Ireland, a flat-rate unlim-ited mileage ticket, valid for rail travel in Europe outside the UK and also the new Eurail Global Pass, which includes countries world-wide. Saver versions are available for those under 26.

Taxis. Most taxis park at designated stands waiting for clients. Many towns have radio-dispatched taxis or online booking, but these usu-ally charge extra for the mileage to pick up the client. Fares can vary from town to town. Dublin and Cork have metered taxis while smaller towns have standard fares or charges by agreement.

Note that you should pay only the charge on the meter plus, if applicable, supplements for extra passengers, additional luggage, waiting time, and trips on public holidays or after midnight. An appropriate tip will be appreciated. Detailed receipts will be provided on request.

Boats and Ferries. With over 4,800km (3,000 miles) of coastline and 14,480km (9,000 miles) of rivers and streams, Ireland is a boater's paradise. You might rent a fishing boat to take advantage of the excellent fresh-water and sea fishing, or enjoy the country's scenic splendours in a rented cruiser (normally available with two to eight berths).

No boating permit is needed for travelling on the Shannon, and all companies offer a free piloting lesson. Points of departure include Carrick-on-Shannon, Athlone, Banagher and Killaloe.

The rugged islands off the coast of Ireland are rich in folklore, antiquities and eye-catching natural wonders (especially birdlife). Fáilte Ireland produces a free brochure, *Explore Islands of Ireland* listing numerous possibilities, including scheduled ferries. This information can also be found at www.discoverireland.ie. The Aran Islands are only a 20 km (30 mile) steamer ride from the Galway coast at Rossaveal, and crossings can also be made in May to September from Doolin in County Clare. Garinish Island, which is noted for its exuberant vegetation, is only 10 minutes away from Glengarriff (County Cork). Bad weather may interrupt ferry services. There are connections to the Aran Islands by air, as well; flights are around 10 minutes.

V

VISAS AND ENTRY REQUIREMENTS

Citizens of many countries do not require visas. EU citizens can enter with a valid passport or national ID card. UK nationals should have a passport or driver's license. See www.dfa.ie for more.

If you are coming from outside the euro zone, you must fill in a

Customs declaration form for cash sums of over €10,000.

The customs restrictions between the Republic and Northern Ireland are normally limited to animals and agricultural products. There are no longer any border security checkpoints but there are selective checks carried out by customs officers.

For more customs regulations information, visit www.revenue.ie.

W

WEBSITES

http://entertainment.ie Find out what's going on.
www.discovernorthernireland.com Northern Ireland Tourist Board.
www.heritageireland.ie Heritage of Ireland.
www.discoverireland.ie Ireland's National Tourism Board.
www.ireland.com Reserve hotels and explore Ireland.
www.visitdublin.com Dublin's official travel and tourism site.
www.visit-belfast.com Official Belfast tourist information.
www.ringofkerrytourism.com The Ring of Kerry: hotels, activities.

Y

YOUTH HOSTELS

The Irish Youth Hostels Association runs 24 hostels in the Republic of Ireland. Membership cards are required to be able to use them and these are issued by national youth hostel associations overseas. An official handbook is available from **An Óige (HO),** 61 Mountjoy Street, Dublin 7; tel: (01) 830 4555; www.anoige.ie. **Independent Hostels of Ireland**, (tel: (74) 973 0130; www.independenthostelsireland.com) is an association of hostel owners with no membership or age requirements and no curfew. There are some 70 hostels throughout Ireland.

There are six youth hostels in Northern Ireland. Ask for details from **Hostelling International Northern Ireland**, 22–32 Donegall Road, Belfast BT12 5JN; tel: (028) 9032 4733; www.hini.org.uk.

RECOMMENDED HOTELS

Price categories below are for a standard double room in high season (some include breakfast – check when you book). Please bear in mind that prices can be much cheaper and deals are often available:

€€€ over €200   £££ over £150
€€ €100–200   ££ £80–150
€ under €100   £ under £80

DUBLIN

Aberdeen Lodge €€ *53-55 Park Avenue, Dublin 4, tel: (01) 283 8155,* www.aberdeen-lodge.com. A large Victorian house in the elegant embassy quarter with quiet, spacious bedrooms beautifully furnished. A five-minute bus or DART ride to the city centre.

Blooms Hotel €–€€ *6 Anglesea Street, Dublin 2, tel: (01) 671 5622,* www.blooms.ie. Located in the Temple Bar area, and like most hotels here, there's a stylish restaurant, bar and basement nightclub to keep you entertained most of the night.

Buswells Hotel €€ *23–27 Molesworth Street, Dublin 2, tel: (01) 614 6500,* www.buswells.ie. Centrally located just opposite the National Museums complex, Buswells is set in a former Georgian townhouse and a favourite haunt of Dublin politicians. Most come just for the restaurant and bar.

Central Hotel €–€€ *1–5 Exchequer Street, Dublin 2, tel: (01) 679 7302,* www.centralhotel.ie. Around for over 100 years and housed in a rambling, refurbished Victorian building with a location as central as its name. The first floor Library Bar attracts literary types.

Clarence Hotel €€€ *6-8 Wellington Quay, Dublin 2, tel: (01) 407 0800,* www.theclarence.ie. Once upon a time this was simply a happy home for clergy up from the country on business. Now it's owned by U2 members and its Octagon bar is one of the most popular meeting places in Dublin. The hotel itself is decked out with Irish craftsmanship that's contemporary yet reminiscent of that country's past.

Clayton Hotel Ballsbridge € *Merrion Road, Dublin 4, tel: (01) 668 1111,* www.claytonhotels.com. An excellent value hotel next to the RDS Arena with over 300 rooms at a flat rate, and a lively lounge bar. Ample car parking onsite, and a five-minute bus or DART ride to the city.

Conrad Dublin €€€ *Earlsfort Terrace, Dublin 2, tel: (01) 602 8900,* www.conraddublin.com. Situated just off St Stephen's Green, the Conrad is the first stop for travelling royalty, though the service seems to roll out the red carpet for all guests. It's most popular for business people but the pub attracts Dubliners.

Dublin International Youth Hostel € *61 Mountjoy Street, Dublin 7, tel: (01) 830 1766,* www.anoige.ie. Budget-priced accommodation in a converted convent.

The Morrison, €€€ *Lower Ormond Quay, Dublin 1, tel: (01) 887 2400,* www.morrisonhotel.ie. City-centre quayside hotel that vies with the Clarence (see above) for title of hippest hotel in town. Contemporary design and good location. A Doubletree by Hilton hotel.

O'Callaghan Davenport Hotel €–€€€ *Merrion Square, Dublin 2, tel: (01) 607 3500,* www.ocallaghanhotels.com. An elegant lemon-coloured building dating from the 1860s and set amidst the attractions of Merrion Square.

The Shelbourne €€€ *27 St Stephen's Green, Dublin 2, tel: (01) 663 4500,* www.theshelbourne.ie. Once home to the Irish Constitution (it was written here), it is now home to Dublin's more distinguished visitors. You couldn't ask for more than a room overlooking St Stephen's Green, but the popularity of the Horseshoe Bar with Dublin's glitterati will give you even more to look at.

Staunton's on the Green €€ *83 St Stephen's Green South, Dublin 2, tel: (01) 478 2300,* www.stauntonsonthegreen.ie. Exclusive Georgian guesthouse overlooking the green with spacious rooms and delightful period decor.

The Westbury €€€ *Grafton Street, Dublin 2, tel: (01) 679 1122,* www.doyle collection.com. A luxury city centre hotel that knows best how to cater to business visitors, though with this location, leisure guests will never need walk far to the city's attractions.

Wynn's Hotel €€ *35–39 Lower Abbey Street, Dublin 1, tel: (01) 874 5131*, www.wynnshotel.ie. This city-centre hotel is just around the corner from the Abbey Theatre.

The Marker Hotel €€€ *Grand Canal Square, Dublin 2, tel (01) 687 5100*, www.themarkerhoteldublin.com. The newest addition to Dublin's luxury hotel scene is slap bang in the middle of the docklands, opposite the Grand Canal Theatre. The building is unapologetically modernist and sleek Head to the rooftop bar for panoramic views of the city.

MEATH

The Millhouse €€€ *Slane, County Meath, tel: (041) 982 0878*, www.themillhouse.ie. Romantic Georgian manor with sumptuous four posters, log fires and the beautiful River Boyne as a backdrop.

CORK

Bellinter House €€€ *Navan, County Meath, tel: (046) 903 0900*,www.bellinterhouse.com. Luxury boutique hotel in a magnificent 18th century country house, set in extensive grounds. Awarding-winning spa and gourmet dining in a cool, informal atmosphere.

Ambassador Hotel €€ *Military Hill, St Luke's, Cork, tel: (021) 453 9000*, www.ambassadorhotel.ie. An imposing Victorian building converted into a stylish, hill-top hotel, with great views of the city and harbour. Both bar and restaurant have a lively local trade.

Ballymaloe House €€€ *Shangarry, Midleton, tel: (021) 465 2531*, www.ballymaloe.ie. One of Ireland's leading country-house hotels, Ballymaloe is a stylishly decorated Georgian house surrounded by the family farm. Renowned for its restaurant, which pioneered the imaginative use of fresh local produce. Children welcome.

Blue Haven Hotel €€ *3 Pearse Street, Kinsale, tel: (021) 477 2209*, www.bluehavenkinsale.com. The hotel's individually-styled rooms are well planned but compact, with the type of space you'd expect in a city-centre hotel. There is a fine bar and coffee shop to retire to, and the location couldn't be better.

Seaview House Hotel €€ *Ballylickey, Bantry Bay, tel: (027) 50073*, www. seaviewhousehotel.com. Set in extensive grounds on the shores of Bantry Bay, this Victorian manor house is now a comfortable, family-run, country-house hotel, with an excellent restaurant. A good base for touring the southwest.

GALWAY

The G Hotel €€€ *Wellpark, Galway, tel: (091) 865200*, www.theghotel. ie. Milliner Philip Treacy has designed a hotel that, like his hats, is quirky, extravagant and luxurious. Kick back in the cool restaurant and bar or chill out in the soothing spa.

Hotel Meyrick €€–€€€ *Eyre Square, Galway, tel: (091) 564041*, www. hotelmeyrick.ie. Historic 19th-century railway hotel located in the heart of the city. There's no lack of old Irish charm here but a swish new makeover means it draws a trendy crowd these days. The Oyster Bar has a wide selection of drinks and an impressive cocktail list.

KERRY

Abbeyglen Castle Hotel €€ *Sky Road, Clifden, Co Galway, tel: (091) 21201*,www.abbeyglen.ie. Stay in an eccentric Irish castle with a parrot presiding over reception. Traditional Irish welcome with great food, a lively bar and a sense of fun throughout.

Greenmount House €€ *Upper John Street, Dingle, tel: (066) 915 1414*, www.greenmounthouse.ie. Only a short walk from the busy town centre, this quiet 14-room guesthouse has a great view of the sunset over Dingle. Rooms are spacious and contemporary and the breakfast is renowned.

Lake Hotel €–€€ *Muckross Road, Killarney, tel: (064) 663 1035*, www.lake hotelkillarney.com. The grounds of this large, rambling, country hotel run right down to the lakeshore and adjoin Killarney National Park, putting you right in the middle of the Killarney experience. There's an outdoor hot tub on the lakeshore, which is part of a fitness centre.

Parknasilla Resort €€€ *Sneem, Ring of Kerry, tel: (064) 667 5600,* www.parknasillahotel.ie. Set in a sheltered inlet with sub-tropical vegetation with a mountain backdrop, this is the ultimate getaway. Excellent pool and spa, old-fashioned lounge and bar, and self-catering options for families.

Sheen Falls Lodge €€€ *Kenmare, tel: (064) 664 1600,* www.sheenfalls lodge.ie. A 120-hectare (300-acre) estate and waterside setting comes along with a room in this lodge. The lounge bar welcomes you in with a roaring fire and gives you a view of the spilling waterfall outside. Spacious rooms offer views of the river or Kenmare Bay. There is also an equestrian centre, library and nature walk through the woodland.

KILKENNY

Club House Hotel €€ *Patrick Street, Kilkenny, tel: (056) 772 1994,* www.clubhousehotel.com. Historic 18th-century hotel; mementoes include a set of witty 19th-century political cartoons.

Hotel Kilkenny €€–€€€ *College Road, Kilkenny, tel: (056) 776 2000,* www.hotelkilkenny.ie. Hotel just outside the city with bedrooms, including some family rooms, in a light, contemporary design.

LIMERICK AND SHANNON

Carlton Castletroy Park Hotel €€–€€€ *Dublin Road, Limerick, tel: (061) 335566,* www.castletroy-park.ie. One of Limerick's most sought after hotels for conference facilities, but still capable of rolling out a proper welcome to leisure guests. Enjoy some relaxation at the Aqua and Fitness club or pamper yourself at the Blue Door Salon.

Dromoland Castle €€€ *Newmarket-on-Fergus, County Clare, tel: (061) 368144,* www.dromoland.ie. This luxury estate can trace its heritage back to Gaelic royalty via the O'Briens, once barons of Inchiquin, who were direct descendants of Brian Boru. Despite all this history, the hotel is welcoming, relaxing and mystical – especially the grounds of the castle which include a lake and delightful parklands.

Fitzgerald's Woodlands House Hotel €–€€ *Knockanes, Adare, County Limerick, tel: (061) 605100,* www.woodlands-hotel.ie. A lively, modern hotel just outside the village, this is a good base for touring the Shannon region. There's a new leisure centre and spa, and a choice of two popular restaurants.

Gregan's Castle €€€ *Ballyvaughan, County Clare, tel: (065) 707 7005* www.gregans.ie. One of Ireland's leading country house hotels in extensive gardens with breathtaking views over Galway Bay. Antique furniture and contemporary art and an outstanding restaurant – but only one TV in the house.

Sleepzone € *The Burren, Doolin Road, Lisdoonvarna, County Clare, tel: (065) 707 4036,* www.sleepzone.ie. This comfortable good value hostel opened in March 2007 in a former hotel in the lively village of Lisdoonvarna.

MAYO

Ashford Castle €€€ *Cong, County Mayo, tel: (094) 954 6003,* www.ash fordcastle.com. The last word in luxury accommodation, this former 19th-century mansion of the Guinness family is arguably Ireland's grandest castle hotel, with parts dating back to the early 13th century. The best rooms are at the top of the castle and offer views of Lough Corrib, the River Cong and the surrounding parkland.

Boffin Lodge € *The Quay, Westport, tel: (098) 26092,* www.boffinlodge. com. Small and stylish traditional-style guesthouse in a tranquil location near Westport's quays, half a mile from the town centre. There are four-poster beds and steam rooms available. Close to a good choice of pubs and restaurants.

The Cong Hostel € *Abbey Street, Cong, County Mayo, tel: (094) 954 6089,* www.quietman-cong.com. The hostel offers budget accommodation located close to pubs, shops, the river and Cong Abbey.

WATERFORD

Granville Hotel €€ *Meagher Quay, Waterford, tel: (051) 305555*, www. granville-hotel.ie. Situated along Waterford's quayside and with as many historical connections as rooms, it's very popular with business travellers but makes a great base for exploring the town.

Richmond House €€ *Cappoquin, County Waterford, tel: (058) 54278*, www.richmondhouse.net. Beautiful country house with spacious rooms and period furnishings set in scenic grounds. Excellent restaurant serving Irish and French cuisine.

Waterford Castle €€€ *The Island, Ballinakill, Waterford, tel: (051) 878203*, www.waterfordcastleresort.com. Historic castle situated on its own private island on the River Suir, surrounded by woodlands and an 18-hole championship golf course. 19 bright and airy bedrooms with stunning views of the estate.

WEXFORD

Ferrycarrig Hotel €€€ *Wexford, tel: (053) 912 0999*, www.ferrycarrighotel.ie. Each of the large, stylish rooms has a view of the River Slaney estuary. Excellent riverside restaurant, bar, spa and leisure activities. Outside Wexford town and convenient for the Irish National Heritage Park.

Kelly's Resort Hotel and Spa €€€ *Rosslare, County Wexford, tel: (053) 913 2114*, www.kellys.ie. Located on sandy Rosslare beach, this is one of Ireland's great family-run hotels, with an excellent restaurant and spa.

NORTHWEST

Green Gate € *Ardvalley, Ardara, County Donegal, tel: (074) 954 1546*, www. thegreengate.eu. This traditional cottage was bought by the proprietor as a writer's retreat. Spend a night atop a hill on the edge of the Atlantic.

Markree Castle €€ *Collooney, Country Sligo tel: (071) 916 7800*, www. markreecastle.ie. Massive castellated mansion on a 400-hectare (1,000-

acre) estate of gardens and parkland that has been in the Cooper family for 350 years; 11km (7 miles) south of town (closed until spring 2017).

Belfast International Youth Hostel £ *22-32 Donegall Road, Belfast BT12 5JN, tel: (028) 9032 4733, www.hini.org.uk.* High-standard hostel in a central location but you don't need a membership card to stay.

Bushmills Inn £–££ *9 Dunluce Road, Bushmills, County Antrim BT 57 8QG, tel: (028) 2073 3000, www.bushmillsinn.com.* This place has all the ingredients of a great Irish holiday – whiskey, comfy beds and great breakfasts – plus the Giant's Causeway is only 3km (2 miles) away. Though refurbished, it still feels like a 19th-century coach house.

Culloden Estate and Spa ££–£££ *142 Bangor Road, Holywood, County Down, tel: (028) 9042 1066, www.hastingshotels.com/culloden-estate-and-spa.* Northern Ireland's most luxurious hotel overlooks Belfast Lough. A glass cabinet lists famous names that have stayed here – they've all signed plastic yellow ducks (each room has one for the bath).

Europa ££–£££ *Great Victoria Street, Belfast BT2 7AP, tel: (028) 9027 1066, www.hastingshotels.com/europa-belfast/.* Next to the Grand Opera House, a 5-minute walk to the Golden Mile. Spacious elegance and stylish comfort.

Malmaison Belfast £££ *34-8 Victoria Street, tel: (028) 9600 1405, www.malmaison.com.* Warehouse conversion near the city centre and the Cathedral Quarter with bordello-themed rooms and art deco-bar.

Ten Square Hotel ££ *10 Donegall Square South, tel: (028) 9024 1001, www.tensquare.co.uk.* A listed Victorian linen warehouse has been transformed into an ultra-luxury hotel with oriental decor and an emphasis on style. Right in the centre of town at Donegall Square.

La Mon Hotel and Country Club ££ *41 Gransha Road, Castlereagh, tel (028) 9044 8631, www.lamon.co.uk.* An oasis of calm that's ideal for families with tennis, swimming, putting green, kids club and babysitting service. Spacious rooms with every modern comfort.

INDEX

INSIGHT ⊙ GUIDES POCKET GUIDE

IRELAND

First Edition 2016

Editor: Kate Drynan; Mary Conneely
Author: Ken Bernstein
Head of Production: Rebeka Davies
Picture Editor: Tom Smyth
Cartography Update: Carte
Update Production: AM Services
Photography credits: Corbis 20, Corrie Wingate/
Apa Publications 4ML, rTL, 5MC, 5MC, 6TL, 6TL,
6ML, 7T, 7TC, 8R, 10, 24, 26, 27, 31, 32, 65, 66,
69, 77, 78, 79, 90, 94, 96, 98, 102, 104, 105; Doug
Plummer 16; Fotolia 4MC, 91; Geary Sweeney
15; Glyn Genin/Apa Publications 4TC, 5M, 8L, 18,
29, 34, 37, 43, 45, 47, 49, 53, 54, 55, 56, 59, 61, 63;
Ireland Tourist Board 5T, 6MC, 9, 13, 38, 40, 52,
70, 72, 74, 88; iStock 51, 103; Kevin Cummins/
Apa Publications 5TC, 5M, 6TC, 7M, 7M, 9R, 80,
81, 82, 83, 84, 86, 92, 100, 106; Richard Nowitz/
Apa Publications 36
Cover Picture: Shutterstock

All Rights Reserved
© 2016 Apa Digital (CH) AG and
Apa Publications (UK) Ltd

Printed in Poland

Distribution
UK, Ireland and Europe: Apa Publications
(UK) Ltd; sales@insightguides.com
United States and Canada: Ingram Publisher
Services; ips@ingramcontent.com

Australia and New Zealand: Woodslane;
info@woodslane.com.au
Southeast Asia: Apa Publications (SN) Pte;
singaporeoffice@insightguides.com
Hong Kong, Taiwan and China:
Apa Publications (HK) Ltd;
hongkongoffice@insightguides.com
Worldwide: Apa Publications (UK) Ltd;
sales@insightguides.com

**Special Sales, Content Licensing
and CoPublishing**
Insight Guides can be purchased in bulk
quantities at discounted prices. We can create
special editions, personalised jackets and
corporate imprints tailored to your needs.
sales@insightguides.com;
www.insightguides.biz

No part of this book may be reproduced,
stored in a retrieval system or transmitted in
any form or means electronic, mechanical,
photocopying, recording or otherwise,
without prior written permission from Apa
Publications.

Contact us
Every effort has been made to provide accurate
information in this publication, but changes are
inevitable. The publisher cannot be responsible
for any resulting loss, inconvenience or injury.
We would appreciate it if readers would call our
attention to any errors or outdated information.
We also welcome your suggestions; please
contact us at: hello@insightguides.com
www.insightguides.com